(14)

THE TR
METAM
IN THE

D0246491

For Bill Stewart, Pip Donaghy and Stephen Williams, who helped create *The Trial* and without whose unfailing belief it would never have seen the light of day.

STEVEN BERKOFF

THE TRIAL
METAMORPHOSIS
IN THE PENAL COLONY

**Three theatre adaptations from
FRANZ KAFKA**

AMBER LANE PRESS

All rights whatsoever in these plays are strictly reserved
and application for performance, etc. must be made
before rehearsals begin to:

Rosica Colin Ltd
1 Clareville Grove Mews
London SW7 5AH

No performance may be given unless a licence has been obtained.

The Trial and *Metamorphosis* first published in 1981 by
Amber Lane Press Ltd.
This edition published in 1988, reprinted 2003 by

Amber Lane Press Ltd
Cheorl House
Church Street
Charlbury, Oxon OX7 3PR
Telephone and fax: 01608 810024
e-mail: info@amberlanepress.co.uk

Printed in Great Britain by Cromwell Press Group,
Trowbridge, Wiltshire

Copyright © Steven Berkoff, 1981, 1988
ISBN 0 906399 84 X

Steven Berkoff on *The Trial*

THE TRIAL is my life. It is anyone's trial. It is the trial of actually creating the production, The Trial. The four months of preparation. I read the book several times before I tried to hew out of its guts its theatrical essence. A metaphysical theatre. I studied it for years and became Joseph K. I was K, struggling in the abyss of self-doubt and yet wanting, like Kafka, to be that man who 'cannot live without a lasting trust in something indestructible within himself.'

It was during a time of deadening theatre work for a hack director that the full force of my energy came throttling out when, after rehearsals, I would escape to the refuge of my room and investigate and unweave the tapestry that was to be my play/ production. It is a diary of a no-one, the diary of the oppressed. I worked on it as a work of obsession feeds inspiration and is its lover. Anything less is a career but for me it was a signpost leading to all the locked-away magician's tricks that I had stored up my sleeve. Kafka expressed me as I expressed Kafka. His words stung and hung on my brain, infused themselves in my art and were regurgitated in my work. The labyrinth. The endless puzzle or the myth of Sisyphus, the quest of Theseus through the maze. Was I Theseus? Joseph K's mediocrity was mine and his ordinariness and fears were mine too: the 'under-hero' struggling to find the ego that would lead him to salvation.

There is a lake of ecstasy that bubbles beneath every shy, ordinary being. What is K's alias Kafka's guilt? Nothing so complex as world guilt or messianic martyrdom, but K's guilt for which he must die is the guilt of betrayal: the guilt of betraying his inner spirit to the safety of mediocrity. For every action that is not expressed through fear, for every desire that wells up in the breast and is not given vent in action through fear turns into a little rat of guilt that gnaws away at your vitals. For every shout held back, for every venture not ventured on, for every regret in the soul, for every compromise you make and slur you took adds to the sorry storehouse of guilt that screams out for justice. The soul screams out for vengeance, starved as it is in its dark and stinking hovel. Guilt is the difference between what your spirit sings out for and what your courage permits you to take. Joseph K's guilt — Kafka's guilt.

'Before the door stands the doorkeeper' is the opening line of the parable related to K by the priest from whom he seeks salvation; and a man is waiting there to gain admission to the Law. The doorkeeper cannot admit him just yet and thus begins the ludicrous parable investigating every contingency and nuance of the Law. An exegesis of vacillation. The man waits for years and years but did not thrust himself through because he believed the doorkeeper when he said that there were other doors and each man guarding them was successively stronger than he. Burst through the doors. But the Law demands due process and one must wait. But in the end he dies of waiting, when the door to the Law was meant only for him. You cannot wait for what is due to you. You must seize it.

We devised a door. A wooden rectangular frame that stood by itself. Ten frames became the set. The set became the environment. A set should be able to melt in an instant and never represent a real heavy piece of pseudo-reality. The theatre of the ultra-bourgeois, so bereft of anything but the obvious, with its expensive lumbering pieces of dead weight. The fortunes spent on trying to be real, to satisfy the bloated after-supper punters. So much waste. Our set of ten screens became the story and as the story could move from moment to moment so could our set — no long waits for scene change but as a flash with the magician's sleight of hand. We could be even quicker than the story. A room could become a trap, a prison, expand and contract and even spin around the protagonist. This enabled us to recreate the environment — both physical and mental — of the book.

To create a metaphysical concept is to condense reality into its surreal intense image: reality heightened by fear, excitement or the pathological hyper-awareness of the artist. The chorus was as a Greek chorus, becoming the conscience of K. The care of their playing, the depersonalized attitude of the people, was necessary for K to view them as a 'faceless group moving together.'

So our actors were a Greek chorus turning a body into a chair or a chest of drawers, since we are what we use. When you search a person's room or cupboard you are violating him since he momentarily becomes the object. The person and his objects are wed, so by taking over the role not only of human but also the environment, the actor is able to be an outraged chest of drawers! So art rules over reality.

THE TRIAL played successfully in Germany to over 1,000 people a night while in London I had to struggle for audiences at the Round House. So THE TRIAL was seen in England for only three weeks, in 1973.

THE TRIAL

The Trial was first performed at the Oval House in London in 1970, and was given its first major production at the Round House in December, 1973 with the following cast:

JOSEPH K	Bill Stewart
BLOCK	Terry McGinity
HULD	Barry Stanton
CHORUS	Hilton McCrea
GUARD	Wolf Kahler
LENI	Teresa Dabreu
MISS BÜRSTNER	Judith Alderson
BAILIFF/PRIEST	Alfredo Michelson
TITORELLI	Steven Berkoff
GUARD/CHORUS	Barry Philips

Directed by Steven Berkoff

The play was first performed in West Germany at the Düsseldorf Playhouse in September, 1976.

TITORELLI: "I got stuck inside a self-portrait!"
(*Photograph: Roger Morton*)

CHARACTERS

JOSEPH K	Chief Clerk at the Bank
MISS BÜRSTNER	Tenant in the Lodging House
MRS GRUBACH	Landlady — and Stripper
TWO GUARDS	Police and Bank Colleagues
DOORKEEPER	Guarding the Great Door of the Law
INSPECTOR	Police
LENI	Huld's Mistress
HULD	The Lawyer of K
K'S FATHER	Disembodied voice of the past
BLOCK	Pathetic Client of Huld's
LAUNDRESS	Works in the Courts
STUDENT	Court Madman and Lover of Laundress
BAILIFF	Works in Courts and is humiliated
THE CHORUS OF NINE PEOPLE WAITING	
TITORELLI	Court Painter — and surrealist verbalist clown
PRIEST	K's Confessor and Judge
A STRANGE MAN	Singer

Plus the clients of Huld — the clerks of the Bank
— the populace of the city

STAGE SETTING

The stage is bare. Ten screens and ten chairs and
a rope are the set. The screens are the structure
of the city — lawcourts, houses and endless corridors. They are a maze and a trap — they are
mirrors and paintings — they are external and
internal worlds. The cast are the environment of
K. The rope is his route as well as his death.

ACT ONE

Electronic Bach plays as the audience enters. Piano, strings: players enter slowly. The CAST *enter one by one — on the stage ten screens are placed — standing upright. The characters relate to each other by formal gestures — they examine the screens. A piano begins a gentle melody which fades with a crashing Bach. A waiting room — flies buzzing. Then the* FIRST VOICE *begins to intone the aphorisms of Kafka.*

VOICE 1: When in this life that demands so mercilessly that we be ready at every moment —

VOICE 2: Can one find a moment to make oneself ready?

VOICE 3: The bony structure of your own forehead blocks the way. You batter yourself bloody on your own forehead.

VOICE 4: From this sense of pain . . . he deduces he is alive.

VOICE 5: Man cannot live without a belief in something indestructible within himself.

[VOICES *humming, growing to wails.*]

VOICE: Before the door stands the doorkeeper.
Before the doorkeeper stands the figure of Joseph K, waiting to gain admittance to the Law.
The doorkeeper says he cannot admit him just yet.
The man asks, "Will I gain admittance later?"
It is possible but not at this moment. However, since the door gapes open as usual, K ventures to peep inside.
"If you are tempted to try and enter without my permission but note that I am powerful . . . and I am only the lowest doorkeeper . . . through the hall is another door through which you must pass and another door through which you must pass and another yet and each man guarding them is successively stronger than I."

The man thinks the Law should be accessible to everyone but on reflection decides to wait . . . He

waits for years . . . He is given a stool . . . He sits
for years exchanging small talk but never is
allowed in. He eventually grows old and his eyes
grow dim . . . He knows not whether his eyes are
deceiving him, or whether the world is growing
darker . . . Yet in all these years of waiting he has
seen no other man seek admittance to the Law
and questions the doorkeeper about this . . . He
beckons the doorkeeper to him as he can no
longer raise his body. The doorkeeper, seeing the
man is near his end, says: "There could be no one
else since the door was intended only for you. I
am now going to shut it . . ."

[*Percussive beat of huge doors shutting.*]

[*Improvisation as* K *walks through tunnels. Names of
characters are called out.*]

K: Leni? Mrs Grubach? I didn't expect to see you
         here . . . Miss Bürstner?

CHORUS: You are charged — charged — in fact arrested.
         Which in turn leads to prosecution — sentence
         — execution. Charged. In fact arrested. [*Repeat as*
         VOICES *echo into distance.*]

K: [*fast*] There must be some mistake — somebody
         must be without question lying about Joseph K
         for I have done nothing wrong in the legal sense.
         Clerical errors can occur — a full stop upside
         down — a decimal point wrongly placed. Mis-
         takes can and relentlessly do happen — I know, I
         work in a bank and know the fallibility of filing
         systems. I represent many people of the highest
         calibre who seek opinions on the most abstruse
         speculations. I could not hold my position
         without trust — although mistakes, though rare,
         occur through no fault of anyone except perhaps
         the negligence of a filing clerk who in the torpor
         of an afternoon's heat mislays a copy of . . .

         I am one of the officials in the Bank. I am alive
         and I'm even envied by the Assistant Manager
         who one night saw me with an important client, a
         famous lawyer; the Manager seemed to think this
         so extraordinary that I should be walking arm in

arm with this lawyer, who he only knows by reputation, that he asked me to sit down. He had to speak to me and I do admit that this was one of the moments that endeared me to him ... moments when the Assistant Manager expressed a certain anxiety for my welfare and my future, although he himself was an over-burdened man. But one of the other clerks in the Bank informed me that this solicitude for me was simply a strategem by which to attach valuable assistants to him for years at the sacrifice of only a few moments of his time. Now, although knowing this pretext to be possibly true, I still felt subjugated [ECHO: *subjugated?*] and completely disarmed. [ECHO: *disarmed?*] I realize this is a weakness but not a crime.

There must be some mistake.
[Speech is repeated very quickly and breathlessly. K *lies down to sleep — the screens that surround him dissolve and return upstage.]*

The City

Sound of ticking of clocks made by the CHORUS. *'Joseph K' sung.*

NARRATOR: It was eight o'clock. The city came to life.
            [Cacophony of city life.]
CHORUS 1:   Someone must have been lying about Joseph K.
CHORUS 2:   For without having done anything wrong ...
CHORUS 3:   He was arrested one fine morning.
CHORUS 4:   His landlady who always brought the breakfast at eight o'clock ...
CHORUS 5:   Failed to appear.
K: That had never happened before.
CHORUS 1:   K waiting a little longer.
CHORUS 2:   People opposite seemed to be staring at him with distinct curiosity.
CHORUS 3:   Then feeling put out and hungry, he rang the bell.

[CHORUS *as bell reaches threatening crescendo.* TWO
GUARDS *enter in bowler hats.*]

GUARD 1:   You rang?

K: I rang for the maid.

GUARD 1:   What's your name?

K: Joseph K.

GUARD 2:   He's the one.

GUARD 1:   Wouldn't you know anyway.

GUARD 2:   Pale as fear.

GUARD 1:   Are you frightened, K?

K: What have I done . . . Why!

GUARD 1:   We're not authorized to tell you that. Proceedings have been instituted against you . . . and
you will be informed of everything in due course.

K: Who are you?

GUARD 2:   We are your friendly warders . . . You're lucky to
have us.

K: What's your name?

GUARD 1:   I'm slim. He's well-knit.

GUARD 2:   I wear a closely fitting black suit.

GUARD 1:   I wear pleats.

GUARD 2:   I wear pockets, buckles and buttons as well as a
belt.

K: They look like tourists.

GUARD 1:   But it's eminently practical.

GUARD 2:   Though we cannot tell you what purpose it
serves.

GUARD 1:   That's who we are and with your kind of luck you
can be very confident.

GUARD 2:   We're exceeding our instructions in speaking to
you so freely.

GUARD 1:   I hope nobody hears me except Frank.

GUARD 2:   Or we would be in trouble with the authorities
whom we represent.

GUARD 1:   We're telling you the truth.
[*Silence.*]

CHORUS 1:   What are they talking about, K?

CHORUS 2:   What authority could they represent?

CHORUS 3:   There is a legal constitution here.

CHORUS 4:   There's no war.

CHORUS 5:   No emergency laws . . .

K:	I have certain legal rights. I demand to know why I am under arrest. You can't just burst in.
GUARD 1:	We can't tell you that. We are merely humble subordinates. Can't you understand? We only obey instructions. Instructions! [*as if having forgotten*] Search the rooms.
	[*Improvisation of searching. Use each other as props, furniture, windows, etc.*]
CHORUS:	[*randomly*] You can't search my room . . . Get out of here . . . Who gave you these instructions . . . ? Nothing in here . . . Mrs Grubach . . . I'll try along here . . . Look, do you have a warrant . . . ? You're under arrest . . . I wonder what's in here . . . A lovely coat . . . I'll try it on . . . How do I look . . . ? Beautiful!
GUARD 2:	Ah, very fancy. We'll take this for now. And the rest of your underwear.
GUARD 1:	If your case turns out all right they will be returned. You never know how long these cases last. And there's a lot of thieving in the depot . . .
GUARD 2:	After a while they sell everything, whether your case is settled or not.
GUARD 1:	Of course you will be compensated.
GUARD 2:	But they pay terrible prices.
GUARD 1:	Much bribery and corruption goes on there.
GUARD 2:	It will be safer with us. OK.
CHORUS 1:	[*to* K] Take it easy.
CHORUS 2:	No need to believe in the worst until it happens . . .
CHORUS 3:	That isn't the right policy here.
CHORUS 4:	It might be a joke concocted by my colleagues for my thirtieth birthday.
K:	Now if I laugh at these men's faces they'll probably laugh with me.
	[K *starts smiling and shaking hands.*]
CHORUS 5:	But it wasn't a joke!
GUARD 1:	Where are your papers?
GUARD 2:	Search him.
K:	What are you looking for? Get away from me. Show me the warrant for my arrest or get out.
GUARD 1:	We can't do that.

GUARD 2:   You mustn't annoy us in the task that we must carry out.

GUARD 1:   We are your friendly warders who will probably stand closer to you than anyone right now.

GUARD 2:   We're just humble subordinates who can scarcely find our way through a legal document.

GUARD 1:   And are only here to guard you ten hours a day and draw our pay. .

GUARD 2:   But we are quite capable of grasping the fact that our authorities . . .

GUARD 1:   Under which we serve . . .

GUARD 2:   Would never demand your arrest without reason.

K: What's the reason?

GUARD 1:   That's for the officials to know who never go hunting for crime in the populace but are drawn toward the guilty and must then send out us warders.

GUARD 2:   That's the law.

CHORUS: Absurd — I've never heard of such a law — did you hear that, Frank? — He doesn't know the law yet he claims to be innocent.

GUARD 2:   You'll never make a man like that see reason.

> [TWO GUARDS *hit* K. *As they hit him* MRS GRUBACH *begins to enter but stops.*]

K: Mrs Grubach. Please come in. Why didn't she come in?

GUARD 1:   What do you want her for?

K: I want my breakfast.

GUARD 2:   Do you hear that? He's starting again.

> [K *is hit again.* MRS GRUBACH *enters — mime putting breakfast on* K*'s back, who is bent double in pain. She exits.*]

GUARD 1:   Honey and toast.

GUARD 2:   Bacon and eggs.

CHORUS: Go out, K. They won't dare stop you — And if they do, it will bring the matter to a head — They'll have to give proper reasons to keep you.

K: But if they did seize me I'd lose my superiority which in a sense I still have.

CHORUS: I feel fit and confident — True, I may miss my work in the Bank this morning — but nobody's making heavy weather of that.

K: Considering the high position I hold there.
CHORUS: Should you give the real reason for your absence?
K: They'd never believe it.
CHORUS: Who *would* believe it?
K: No. The best course to take is to follow the natural train of events. Do nothing and see what transpires.

Inspector arrives

VOICE: [*loudly*] Joseph K!
[*Screens change to long corridors through which* INSPECTOR *travels.*]
K: At last.
[*He starts to move.*]
GUARD 1: Not yet. Not like that.
GUARD 2: Smarten yourself up.
GUARD 1: Comb your hair.
K: Leave me alone.
GUARD 2: Should have had a bath.
GUARD 1: No time for that.
GUARD 2: Put on a black coat.
CHORUS: [*calls*] Joseph. Joseph K. Mr K.
INSPECTOR: Ah. Mr K. I imagine you were surprised by this morning's visit.
K: Certainly I'm surprised.
CHORUS: K was filled with pleasure having discovered a sensible man at last.
K: But I am by no means very surprised.
INSPECTOR: Not very surprised?
K: Perhaps you misunderstand me — I mean . . . May I sit down?
INSPECTOR: It's not usual.
K: I mean, of course I'm surprised, but when one has struggled alone for thirty years in this world as I have you become hardened to surprises — and don't take them too seriously — particularly this morning.
INSPECTOR: Why this morning?
K: Look, I don't say that the whole thing has been a joke, I don't say that — I mean it would be a

pretty complex joke — yes . . . ? I mean the whole staff of the boarding house would have to be involved — right? — as well as your people — so I don't think it's a joke.

INSPECTOR: It's no joke.

K: On the other hand, it can't be very serious either — since I can't recall the slightest offence that might be charged against me but even that's of no importance — the real question is: who accuses me? *Who? — what of? what authority?* Are you really police? Where's your uniform? You don't call that a uniform, it's more like an outfit for the firemen's ball.

[CHORUS *giggles.*]

INSPECTOR: Silence!

K: Gentlemen, I only want a clear explanation, settle that, then we can go . . .

INSPECTOR: You're labouring under a great illusion — I can't tell you anything because we don't know — we don't know what you have done or who accuses you — all we can tell you is you're arrested — that's our job — that's why we're here — However, I can give you some advice.

K: Yes.

INSPECTOR: Think more — talk less. Don't go on about how innocent you are. Besides being boring, it makes a bad impression. It's what you . . . It's what you can do that counts.

K: [*Walks up and down, uncertain what to do.*] I want to phone my lawyer. May I?

INSPECTOR: Go ahead. But I don't see the sense in that.

K: You don't see the sense in that! What kind of man are you? You and your rednecks. They burst in here, turn clowns upside down, act like a couple of clowns from a third-rate variety act, arrest me, no reason given, and when I want to phone my lawyer to ask him — *What in God's name is the meaning of this . . . ?* you say there's no sense in it.

[*During this speech pictures are being taken of* K, *as if by reporters.*]

INSPECTOR: [*after a silence*] All right, phone.

K: I don't want to now.
INSPECTOR: Please do.
K: I said I don't want to.
             [CHORUS *have edged round again, faces appearing
             from behind screens.*]
             Enjoying the Show! Go away! [*Faces disappear.*] Come
             gentlemen, the best thing we can do is to forget
             the whole thing — who's right or wrong —
             obviously the whole thing has been a mistake —
             you've got the wrong man. Let's settle the whole
             affair by shaking hands.
CHORUS: He steps over the Inspector — holds out his hand
             — the Inspector raises his eyes and bites his lip
             — stares at the proffered limb — K still believes
             he is going to close with the offer but . . .
INSPECTOR: No — no, that really can't be done. It's not that
             simple, but don't give up hope — why should
             you? — you're under arrest, that's all — I was
             asked to inform you of this — that's done and I've
             observed your comments — that's enough for
             now anyway, and we can say goodbye and you
             can go to work.
K: How can I go to the Bank if I'm under arrest?
INSPECTOR: You don't understand — being arrested won't
             interfere with your going about your everyday
             life.
K: Then being arrested isn't so bad?
INSPECTOR: Who said it was?
K: In that case why inform me of it if it makes no
             difference?
INSPECTOR: It's my duty.
K: A stupid duty.
INSPECTOR: That may be — I'm not forcing you to go to the
             Bank. I'm assuming you'd want to, and to help
             you make your late arrival less noticeable, I
             detained your colleagues to take you back.
CHORUS: Goodbye sir. Goodbye sir. Goodbye sir.
             [*Street noises. Traffic sounds. They mime taxi ride.
             They speak without communicating to each other.
             Screens re-adjust — K and* GUARDS *step through
             them.*]
K: I didn't recognize you before.

CLERKS: [*as they ride*] How could he fail to recognize us? — his insignificant anaemic colleagues — the stiff Rabenstein and Kullich with his revolting smile caused by a chronic muscular twitch.

K: I'm glad to be getting to work at last.

CLERKS: We were waiting a long time.

K: That Inspector confused me or I would have recognized them.

CLERK 1:   He doesn't seem to show much presence of mind.

CLERK 2:   Or we're too subordinate employees to be recognized.

K: I must be careful from now on to keep my wits alert. You know, strange as it may seem, this is just the moment when I really would have liked a friendly chat with them.

CLERKS: But suddenly we were tired.

CLERK 1:   And I can only face him with my nervous grin.

CLERK 2:   Which, unfortunately, on the grounds of humanity, could not be made the subject of light conversation.

The Bank

Traffic stops, screens re-shape into long office. CAST *becomes the office of a busy bank, machinery, people walking robot-like. Typists use their heads as typewriters. People move quickly, avoiding each other with clockwork precision.*

TYPISTS: Good morning, Mr K. [*Repeated several times in various tones.*]

K: Good morning.

VOICES: Hello, can I help you?

You're welcome.

Thank you.

You're welcome.

Can I help you? [*etc.*]

     [K *gets involved when he finds suitable space, becoming part of one vast machine. Silence.*]

VOICES: Happy birthday, Mr K.

     [*Silence.*]

K: [*embarrassed*] I thank you. I'd just like to say on the occasion of my thirtieth birthday . . .

[VOICES *talking — bank business continues.* K *is ignored. The noise builds to a crescendo interrupted by loud phone ringing.*]

CLERK: Telephone, Mr K.

[CLERKS *act out phone, making a long line. One caller on either side.*]

VOICE: Hello, Joseph K? — Forgive me for interrupting you at your work — your investigation is proceeding normally — since we wish to disturb you as little as possible we thought Sunday might be a convenient time to hold interrogations. If not, we can conduct them at night, but then probably you would not be fresh enough. Of course, it is understood that you must appear without fail.

K: What happens if I don't come?

VOICE: We shall know where to find you. You are to report to 14 Julia Street.

[*Peeps of coins running out. Caller puts new coin in which is swallowed up by box, or similar effect depending on country this is played in.*]

VOICE: Did you hear that, Mr K? You are to report to 14 Julia . . .

[*He hangs up.*]

K: What name? I'm cut off.

CLERK: Shall I get him back for you?

K: He didn't leave his number.

CLERK: Then I can't get him back.

K: No.

[*Office continues as before. Loud bell rings. Everybody stops work. People leave.*]

ALL: Goodnight, Mr K.

[*Scene dissolves.*]

NARRATOR: That spring K had been accustomed to passing an evening with a few drinks and once a week visited a girl called Elsa who gave occasional performances.

[*Music of stripper, sudden, loud, raucous. A voice introducing* ELSA *(the one, the only, etc.).* ELSA *does a strip. Music suddenly stops. She almost seduces him until . . .*]

NARRATOR: But tonight he resolved to go straight home.
[*Groans from all the men. Scene changes abruptly and stripper becomes* MRS GRUBACH.]
[*Thus we see his expectations and then the reality.*]

The Lodging House of Mrs Grubach

MRS G: Evening, Joseph. [*She is sitting.*]
K: Still working, Mrs Grubach?
MRS G: There's a lot to do.
K: I'm sorry to bother you so late. I should apologize for today — giving you all that extra work. I mean those men who came this morning.
MRS G: Didn't bother me in the least.
K: She seems surprised that I mention it at all. Seems to think that it's not quite right to talk about it — all the more reason why I should — it might have given you much more work, but it won't happen again.
MRS G: No, it won't happen again.
K: Do you really think that?
MRS G: Yes Joseph, and you mustn't take it to heart. [*She sews button on* K, *and continues to fuss about him.*] Lots of strange things happen in the world. I must admit, since you've been so frank with me, that I listened behind the door, and these two men told me a few things. Not all bad. You're under arrest certainly but not for anything criminal. You're not a thief or something like that. It's something special with you. Something almost learned about your arrest. Am I talking stupidly, Mr K?
K: No, Mrs Grubach. No! I agree with you. I was unprepared. I didn't want to speak about it, but I wanted your opinion. And I'm glad we're in agreement. Let's shake on it.
MRS G: [*ignoring his hand*] Don't take it so much to heart.
K: I had no idea I was taking it so much to heart. [*Awkward silence.*] Is Miss Bürstner in?
MRS G: No . . . she's at the theatre. Still working. Shall I give her a message?

K:　Oh no. I only wanted to apologize. Those men searching her room today.

MRS G:　There's no need — everything's just as it was. All put back nice and tidy. You know she's often late, still, young people are like that.

K:　Certainly. But it can go too far.

MRS G:　How right you are. I've nothing against her. She's a dear good kind girl. Decent, punctual, industrious, full of good qualities, except . . .

K:　Except what?

MRS G:　I shouldn't say it — but I've seen her with a different man twice already this month.

K:　So?

MRS G:　It worries me terribly. I can't sleep for waiting up for her and that's not the only thing. I've been suspicious of her for a long time now.

K:　You're wrong . . . You're quite mistaken. You misunderstood my remark about her. It wasn't meant in any way, and I must warn you about saying anything about her. There isn't a word of truth in what you say.

MRS G:　Oh please don't go. I didn't mean to offend you. You're the only one I've spoken to. After all, I must keep the house respectable.

K:　Respectable! If you want to keep your house respectable you can begin by giving me your notice.

MRS G:　[*upset*] Oh Joseph! You know I'd never give you notice. You've known me long enough. Don't say such a thing.

K:　Please, Mrs Grubach. You'll wake the whole house. I didn't mean what I said. We misunderstood each other, that's all. It can happen between friends.

[MRS GRUBACH *takes her chair and begins to leave. Pause.*]

I'm free. But I'm under arrest.

MRS G:　They don't arrest you for nothing.

K:　What do you mean about being drawn toward the guilty?

MRS G:　They get arrested and don't know why. After all, I

must keep my house respectable in the interest of
my lodgers.

[LODGERS *are seen through their screens during this
scene as if through invisible walls and each involved in
his own small actions.*]

The Lodgers of Mrs Grubach

K *begins walking through the lodging house calling for*
MISS BÜRSTNER. THE LODGERS *as if in parody move
from their screens — tapping is heard — they change rooms
— screens move places — the events of night take place
invisibly — women are seduced — the lonely listen —
creaking sounds, sound of orgasms. The effect is of a mad
house. A* VOICE *shouts.*

VOICE: Quiet!

[THE LODGERS *return to their original positions.*]

Miss Bürstner

CHORUS: Eleven o'clock struck.

[MISS BÜRSTNER *appears. She takes eleven steps to
reach her room. She starts undressing.* K *takes the same
route to her room, appears to look in keyhole. Whispers.*]

K: Miss Bürstner. Miss Bürstner.
CHORUS: It was said like a prayer.
MISS B: What is it?
K: Me, Joseph K. I'd like to speak to you.
MISS B: Right now?
K: I've been waiting over an hour. [*fast*] I've no
             special desire to see her, I can't even remember
             what she looks like and I've put off my visit to
             Elsa this evening because of her, apart from
             missing my supper too . . . it's about something
             that happened today.
MISS B: Oh well. Come in. You'll wake the whole house
             up. [*He enters.*] Well, what is it? You've made me
             curious now.

K: Oh, I know you'll say it could have waited, it's not that urgent.

MISS B: Get to the point.

K: That's just what I'll do. I want to apologize for this morning. Some people searched your room.

MISS B: My room?

> [*As* MISS B *listens, she mimes the taking off of clothes, performed by* CHORUS *as artifacts in the room.*]

K: Strange people against my will.

MISS B: *Well!*

K: That's so.

MISS B: Anyway, you've apologized — and the room looks undisturbed. So I forgive you.

K: But I haven't come to the important bit.

MISS B: Oh, there's more?

K: I was arrested this morning.

MISS B: No!

K: Yes!

MISS B: Oh, how exciting. Why you?

K: Exactly. Why me? You think I must be innocent, eh?

MISS B: I don't like to commit myself — just like that. I don't know you, do I? It could be a serious crime — yet you're free right now. You don't look like you've just escaped. So I presume it's not serious.

K: No, it's not serious, but they suspect me of something.

MISS B: I see.

K: Have you had any legal experience?

MISS B: Not legal, no . . . I'd like to though, law courts are terribly interesting. The law has a special attraction to me. In fact I'm taking a job in a law office next week.

K: Then perhaps you can help me in my trial.

MISS B: Why not? I'd love to be of use.

K: I mean, it doesn't mean a lawyer.

MISS B: Just some advice?

K: Exactly.

MISS B: Then tell me what it's about.

K: I don't know. That's the trouble. I don't know myself. I was just arrested. No interrogation. Nothing. They just poured in.

MISS B: What was it like?
        [She relaxes, adopting a very seductive position, which disturbs K.]

K: Horrible. You're taken completely by surprise. *I wish she'd change her position. I can't concentrate.*

MISS B: Yes, but what happened?

K: I'll show you — but I need to move about a bit.

MISS B: What on earth for?

K: So you'll understand.

MISS B: Well, if you need to for your performance.

K: I have to, to show you where the various people are.

        [Lights change. Actors appear ready to perform the scene as K demands. It should be explicit that what is seen goes on only in K's head and is not seen in the same way by MISS B. The actors will perform and improvise the scene in a perfunctory way.]

K: Now this morning, Mrs Grubach didn't bring me my breakfast. Strange for her, so I rang the bell and in they come. Two of them. Oh, to set the scene properly, a white blouse is dangling on the window latch. Anyway, these two come in, one great huge ape of a man and another a tiny dwarf-like creature. They started to search. They went through the cupboards. They went through the drawers, they even looked under the window ledge. But I had nothing to hide so what were they looking for? Then they started to search me. Now I may seem timid to you, Miss Bürstner, but I assure you I'm not. I allow no one to walk over me. A quick elbow into the stomach for the big one, and the little one saw the power of my left coming and scuttled his way off into the corner. Then on floated this great Inspector. Huge pompous man he was. Oh, you've never seen such pomposity in all your life. Well, of course, with the police in the building the neighbours couldn't keep their noses out of it. No, there they were, scuffling about on the landings, on the stairs, in and about the rooms discussing my

affairs. Anyway, the Inspector comes right up to
me and says . . .

INSPECTOR: *Joseph K!* Do you realize what time it is?

K: Pardon?

INSPECTOR: You're keeping everybody awake.

LODGERS: And I have to get up early in the morning.
Are you all right, Miss Bürstner?
We thought he was disturbing you.
I'll get the police!

[*They exit, mumbling various complaints.*]

MISS B: Everybody's heard us, you fool.

K: I'm sorry. I'll put everything right.

MISS B: Go quickly. Hurry up and go, they're all
listening.

K: You're not angry with me?

MISS B: No, I'm never angry.

K: You're sure?

[*He attempts to kiss her but fails awkwardly. He is left
straddled over a chair.*]

I wanted to call her by her first name — but I
didn't know what it was.

[*Grumbles from* LODGERS *heard. Screens re-arranged
to show* K's *room — in other words room goes to* K
rather than K *goes to his room.*]

That Inspector confused me. Oh, they had to
come here, it can't be the Bank. At the Bank they
have secretaries, clerks, officers . . . Telephones
ringing all the time. Clients queuing, waiting for
appointments. At the Bank you're on your toes.
They would never have caught me out there . . .

[K *uses screen as mirror — a figure on the reverse side
pulls him through — he witnesses the next scene as from
the other side of limbo — the whipping takes place first
— the text follows as a separate section.*]

The Whipper

TWO GUARDS *appear as if transported by* WHIPPER.

K: What are you doing here?

GUARD 1:   So, we're going to be flogged because you de-
nounced us.

GUARD 2:   You said we stole your linen.

GUARD 1:   Of course we shouldn't have, but if you knew how little they pay us.

GUARD 2:   It's a tradition that the warders keep shirts and linen.

GUARD 1:   Because it's no use to you once you've been arrested — I have a family to feed and Frank wants to get married.

GUARD 2:   Why did you denounce us?

GUARD 1:   We would have been promoted to whippers pretty soon, but for your confession.

K: I only told Miss Bürstner.

GUARD 1:   The Law found out — our careers are ruined and now we have to take this terrible beating.

K: Is it painful?

GUARD 2:   Painful? It's terrible — terrible!

WHIPPER: *Shut up!* Fear of the whip is driving them mad. [*He starts whipping.*]

K: Stop! I'll pay you to let them go.

WHIPPER: You can't bribe me. I'm an official of the court. It pays me to whip and I whip.

GUARD 1:   Oh Mr K, sir. Try and get me off. Frank is older than I am and less sensitive. He's had a small whipping years ago — but my record is clean. Oh please, Mr K. My fiancée is waiting for me — she'll be so ashamed.

K: They're not guilty. The guilt lies with the whole organization. It's the high officials who are guilty. Let's whip them. I'd even help you. Leave them. Whip me instead. I'll take off my clothes and offer myself. There you are if you need a sacrifice.

    [*Wailing* VOICES.]

    [*startled*] I must try to sleep.

The City

CHORUS *sings 'Joseph Joseph K'.*

CHORUS: It was eight o'clock. [*Sound of alarm clocks.*] Sunday morning.

K: Oh my God. My interrogation.
[K *rushes into a train which is formed by the group, strap-hanging citizens of the metropolis. Train sounds, sounding like 'Joseph K' being repeated.*]
I wonder when I get a summons.

VOICES: Enquiries must take place first.
They will follow each other more and more regularly as time goes on.
The interrogation must be very thorough.
Bad news, K?

K: No, no, everything's fine.

ASST. MAN.: Hello K. Would you like to go to a party on my yacht this Sunday? There will be some very influential people there.

K: Sorry, I have a previous engagement.

ASST. MAN.: Pity . . . pity.

VOICE: The Assistant Manager asked him to a party on a yacht!

VOICE: How important K is in the Bank.

K: It's just that my friendship is valuable to the Assistant Manager.

ASST. MAN.: I humbled myself by inviting him though I only dropped it casually.

K: My case is under way. I must fight it. The first interrogation must be the last.

VOICE: It may be the first of many.

K: They hung up and didn't tell me who to ask for.

VOICE: Shall I get them back for you?

K: They didn't leave me the number.

VOICE: Then I can't get them back for you.

VOICE: You are to report to 14 Julia Street.

K: What street is this?

VOICE: It's Julia Street.

VOICE: You're there, K.

K: Ah!

CHORUS: [*Speaking in matter-of-fact tones.* CAST *enact briefly almost a series of still shots, or quick images in counterpoint to* CHORUS.] Being Sunday morning the houses were occupied by people in shirt sleeves. [*Image.*]
Women throng in and out of the small grocery shops. [*Image.*]
A fruit hawker peddles his wares. [*Image.*]

An old tune is being murdered by an organ grinder. [*Image.*]
K penetrated deeper into the street. [*Image.*]
He hopes the magistrate might be leaning out of the window and can witness that K is on his way. He stops and examines a house with close attention. [*Image.*] *Yes! It's number fourteen!*
K sees a staircase and decides to chance it.
He's going up the stairs — he's uncertain but feels a strange pull in the direction he's going.
     [CHORUS *create stairs.*]

K: If what the guard said was right about the attraction existing between law and guilt, it follows that the Court of Enquiries must be in the direction I choose.

NARRATOR: Is K right in his judgement or was the guard speaking the truth or could they both be wrong? K reaches the first floor. He could not really ask for the Court of Enquiry yet he wants to see the rooms. He invents a carpenter called . . .

K: Lanz.

CHORUS: The first name that comes into his head.

K: Does the carpenter Lanz live here?

VOICE: Never heard of him.

K: Does carpenter Lanz live here?

VOICE: Who? Not here.

VOICE: Not here either.

     [*The screens become doors opening and closing. Contracting and surrounding him — he peers inside — the occupants are of a tenement in the poor quarter of a city. They dissolve and form a circle — the* CAST *leave, and group on chairs surrounding the action —* THE LAUNDRESS *uses the screens to 'hang' her washing on.*]

The Laundress

LAUNDRESS *comes downstairs and mimes washing. She is voluptuous — earthy — obviously attractive to* K.

LAUNDRESS: There's no carpenter called Lanz.

K: It was a trick.

LAUNDRESS: So you could snoop around.

K: I wasn't given the name.

LAUNDRESS: You could have asked for the Courts — you were shy — in case people thought you were a criminal.

K: You're clever.

LAUNDRESS: I have to be. I'm the laundress. My husband is a court bailiff. Would you like me to say something to the examining magistrate for you?

K: You know him?

LAUNDRESS: Of course, we live here rent free, as long as we clear out when the cases are on. [*Takes his hand.*] You're arrested, aren't you?

K: I stand accused, yes. Why? Do you think you can help me?

LAUNDRESS: I'd love to. It's so horrible here, you might be able to improve things.

K: I'm not here to improve anything, except my own case.

LAUNDRESS: [*seductive*] How shall I help you?

K: Quick, show me the law records. We'll see once and for all what I'm charged with.
[*The actors become* FIGURES *in the screens which become a large book of dirty pictures.*]
It's full of pictures, just pictures. Here's a man and woman sitting naked on a sofa.

LAUNDRESS: They are mostly dirty books.

K: And that's what these fine men of the law read, who sit in judgement on us?
[FIGURES *in mime book search for each other.*]

FIGURE 1: Greta, where are you?

FIGURE 2: I'm on page two.

FIGURE 1: Come here you naughty girl —
[*They chase each other through the book and exit.*]

LAUNDRESS: Come and sit next to me. You have lovely dark eyes. I've been told that I have lovely eyes too, but yours are much lovelier.

K: [*to* AUDIENCE] So this is what it amounts to. She's offering herself to me. She's corrupt like the rest of them. She's bored here and makes up to any stranger who takes her fancy with compliments

about his eyes. [*to* LAUNDRESS] If there's no
session I may as well go.

LAUNDRESS: Don't go away please. You mustn't go away with
the wrong idea about me. Please stay a little
longer. Please.

K: How do you know the magistrate? If you really
want to help me you have to know the officials.

LAUNDRESS: Oh I do! The magistrate likes me. Last Sunday he
came to my room in the middle of the night. I
woke up and found him standing by the bed.

K: Where was your husband?

LAUNDRESS: In bed with me, of course.

K: What did your husband say?

LAUNDRESS: Nothing. He's a deep sleeper. He didn't wake up.

K: That's terrible.

LAUNDRESS: I was so startled. I almost screamed but the
magistrate was very kind and he said he would
never forget the picture I made lying asleep in
bed.

K: Aaah!

LAUNDRESS: And yesterday he bought me some stockings.
They're beautiful ... look ... the magistrate
takes a great interest in me, and I have a great
influence over him. He gave them to the student
to give to me.

K: Who is the student?

LAUNDRESS: Don't be angry but he's my lover. I have no
choice. He's very powerful in the Courts, otherwise we'd have no home to stay in. Every time the
Court's in session, we have to take all our furni-
ture out and put it all back again on Sundays and
sometimes the sessions last until late in the
evening. Oh God. He's watching us.

[STUDENT *is seen in the background beckoning her.*]
I'm coming, Burtold.

[*The screens are also removed which are their protection.*]

K: Don't go.

LAUNDRESS: I must. Forgive me. He's so ugly but I must go
with him. I have no choice. I'll be back in a little
while and I'll go with you wherever you want.

[STUDENT *picks her up and throws her over his shoulder.*]

And you can do whatever you like with me . . . If only I could get out of here forever.

[STUDENT *has put her down and attempts to make love to her. K tries to stop them but doesn't succeed. His attempts are feeble. He is helpless. They whisper and kiss as if he is not even touching them.*]

K: I'll take you from them. *My God, she's so attractive. Soft and warm.*

CHORUS: Perhaps she's a trap, K.

K: I don't care. In what way can she entrap me? There's nothing the Courts can do, anyway, how could she trap me? I'll take that risk. I don't care about my case. I'll get a good laugh out of it. Do you hear me? A good laugh. Ha! Ha! Ha! That's if it ever comes to court, which I doubt. Then one day the dirty old magistrate will tiptoe into her room after making up some more lies about me and find her bed empty . . . empty because she's gone off with me.

[K *grabs her arm. This is the first time he is noticed. They have a tug of war with her.*]

That supple, voluptuous, warm body under that dress belongs to me and me alone.

STUDENT: Go away. There's nothing to stop you — you won't even be missed. In fact it was your duty to vanish as soon as you saw me.

K: I hear you are a student.

STUDENT: So?

K: Then you've a long way to go before becoming a judge.

[*Bravo and cheers from the crowd.*]

STUDENT: You shouldn't be allowed to move around at large like that. He should be put under house arrest . . . between interrogations . . . I told the magistrate that.

[K *tries to snatch the* LAUNDRESS.]

K: Come away.

STUDENT: Oh no, you won't get her.

[*He lifts her up again.*]

LAUNDRESS:	It's no use. This little monster won't let me go.
K:	You don't want to be free.
LAUNDRESS:	No, no, you don't understand. He's only taking me to the examining magistrate.
	[K *still attempts to get hold of her. She is passed around, always just avoiding* K, *who eventually tires and gives up.*]
K:	I wish I'd never seen you. I'd like to see that bandy, creeping slug of a student, that puffed up nothing, kneeling by Elsa's bed, begging for it, wringing his hands, tongue hanging out.
CHORUS:	This picture pleased K so much that he decided if ever the opportunity came to take the student along to see Elsa . . .
K:	I don't even believe she was going to the examining magistrate. It's all a part of their plot to take you off guard.
	[BAILIFF *suddenly appears as if he has been running at top speed on the spot. He enters through revolving screens. Image of perpetual running.*]
BAILIFF:	You haven't seen my wife, have you?
	[*He asks the same question to everyone around and they all respond negatively.*]
K:	Are you the bailiff?
BAILIFF:	Yes . . . ah! You're the defendant K. I see it in your lips. [*Holds out his hand.*]
K:	Your wife has just been carried off by the student. I was just speaking to her a moment ago.
BAILIFF:	Oh no! And today's Sunday too! They're always carrying her away from me, even on my day off. I'm not supposed to work today. So they send me out on a useless errand, just to get me out of the way. But they never send me too far, just to give me a little hope of getting back in time . . . if I hurry. So I run as fast as I can. Just to save time, you know, and run back again at top speed. And yet that student always gets here first. He hasn't so far to go, you see. If I wasn't so worried about losing my job, I'd have crushed that student against the wall long ago. I dream about it daily. I can see him flattened out, squashed flat, arms

and legs nailed down, writhing and spurting blood . . . But it's only a dream.

K: Is there no other remedy?

BAILIFF: None. And it's getting worse. Till now only the student had her, and now he's carrying her off to the magistrate. Everybody's having her.

K: You think she may enjoy it?

BAILIFF: Of course she does; she loves it. Laps it up. My wife is the best-looking woman in the place. What can I do?

K: If that's how it is, there's nothing you can do.

BAILIFF: I can't touch that student. He's too influential. That's why nobody will do it for me. But a man like you could do it.

K: Why me?

BAILIFF: You're under arrest . . . you've nothing to lose.

K: What do you mean?

BAILIFF: All cases are a foregone conclusion.

K: Not in this case they're not. Anyway, I'll do what I can about the student.

BAILIFF: I really would be very grateful to you.

> [VOICE *over loudspeaker is heard:* 'Will the BAILIFF *please report upstairs'.*]

I must report upstairs now. Would you like to come? Follow me.

K: I've no business there.

BAILIFF: You can see the defendants waiting. You're not the only one who is accused. They're all accused, all waiting.

> [*They go through a series of passages. Two men form the architecture of the building by using a long rope which stretches across the stage. They create a series of angles indicating their journey.*]

K: The Court must be in a bad state to hold their offices in a tenement. Not likely to inspire much respect from an accused man. But probably the officials pocket any money before it could be used for purposes of the law.

> [BAILIFF *mutters acknowledgements.*]

Now I can understand why they had chosen to

molest me at work and at home. They're too
ashamed to summon me here.

> [*Their journey gets faster and faster, going upstairs and
> downstairs as* K *continues his preamble. Eventually it
> resembles a race.*]

CHORUS: And it's the Bailiff in the lead from K. K is
catching up and now it's K and the Bailiff. The
Bailiff and K. K is sneaking ahead. He's leading
by a short neck. Bailiff moving up fast behind
him, it's anyone's race . . . Ladies and gentlemen, K is now moving ahead by a length, in very
fit condition. Bailiff is trailing behind now, and
it's K!

> [*At the end of the race the rope has become the finishing
> line.* CHORUS *cheer. Men with rope become part of the
> waiting mob.*]

The Offices of the Court

The CHORUS *as* DEFENDANTS. *They are trapped inside
their screens, arms outstretched. They step from side to side
like playing cards — one behind the other.*

CHORUS: [*sung*] There are just a few of us today. Because
it's Sunday. [*repeated*]
> [*As* K *speaks,* CHORUS *form long corridor of fearful*
> DEFENDANTS.]

K: Why are you waiting here?
VOICE 1: I'm waiting for papers I have submitted.
K: Why are you waiting, sir?
VOICE 2: I've only got one more question to answer.
K: Why are you waiting here?
VOICE 3: I'm waiting for an affidavit.
K: Are the affidavits really necessary?
VOICE: *No.*
VOICE: *Yes.*
VOICE 4: Mr K. I can tell you why you're waiting here, Mr
K. You are waiting here because you have to . . .
K: Why are you waiting here?
VOICE 5: I'm not like the others. I came by car. I have an
appointment here at ten o'clock.

VOICE:	It's eleven!
VOICE 5:	He's late.
VOICE 4:	Mr K. Sir. I do remember now. It's so obvious I keep forgetting. Mr. K. You are waiting for exactly the same reason . . .
VOICE:	He always forgets.
	[*Chatter begins from everyone giving their reasons and excuses.*]
K:	*Will you listen to me!*
	[*He takes hold of one of the accused.*]
VOICE:	Tell him not to shout like that.
VOICE:	What does he want?
VOICE:	He'll bring the officials down on us.
VOICE:	They'll demand an official explanation for his presence.
VOICE:	His grip felt like iron pincers instead of fingers.
K:	That's ridiculous. If you don't believe I'm under arrest I'll be on my way.
VOICE:	You'll have to wait like all of us.
VOICE:	Some of us have been waiting for years.
K:	[*weaker*] I'm an accused man like all of you. I only want to know the date of my interrogation.
VOICE:	Perhaps he's come out of curiosity.
VOICE:	To see us withering here.
VOICE:	Or to spy.
VOICE:	Curiosity leads to spying.
	[CHORUS *take up cry of 'Spy, Spy'.*]
K:	I must go. How does one get out of here?
BAILIFF:	[*moving into the group*] You're not lost. Remember the way you came. Go along the corridor. Turn right and follow the lobby. You can't miss it.
	[*Group turn themselves into a corridor. As* K *moves down it they change position, creating a maze.*]
VOICE:	No K, it's this way.
VOICES:	Straight through.
	Turn left.
	Turn right.
	Go back.
	That's the wrong way.
	Through here.
	Back to the beginning.
	[*Movement speeds up, throwing him backwards and*

forwards like a drunken man. Screens start to spin — a stroboscope freezes the action. At the end K *collapses, having been thrown through time. Now he finds himself in a waiting room.*]

GIRL: May I help you? You feel a little dizzy, don't you? [*She speaks to him as if to herself.*] Her face was close to his now and wore that serene look that many women have in the first flower of their youth. Will you help me carry him to the sick room? Will you help me please?

SMART MAN: I fancy, said the man who was stylishly dressed and was wearing a conspicuously smart grey waistcoat, ending in two long sharp points, that the gentleman's sickness is due to his long stay here and that what he would really like best is not to be taken into the sickroom at all, but out of these offices altogether.

K: Yes, that's it. I should feel better at once. Oh I'm used to a stuffy office. I work in one myself, but this is too much. I'm not so weak. Not really. Just a little support under the arms and I'll be fine.

SMART MAN: You see. It's only here that he feels ill. Not anywhere else. But of course I'll show the gentleman the way out.

GIRL: Don't let his laughter bother you. He's really very clever since he's our information chief, and helps our clients with their problems, since our procedure is not well-known among the populace. Go on, ask him a question. He has an answer for everything. That's why he's smarter than any of us.

SMART MAN: Do you have to tell him our secrets?

GIRL: I had to explain why you laughed. You might have upset him.

SMART MAN: [*to* GIRL] Do you want to go back to where you came from?

K: I must go. I really must go.

SMART MAN: He wants to go but makes no attempt to move. You tell him a hundred times where the door is and he just stays there.

GIRL: Would you like to stay here?

K: No. I . . . don't want . . . a . . . rest . . .

NARRATOR:	K saw he was standing before the open door. All his energies returned in an instant to gain a foretaste of Freedom. His feet are already on the stairs. Wait, no! Thank them, K. Shake hands with them. That's right, with all of them. You may need them again, you may need to go back there. Now go. Hurl yourself down the stairs. You stride down the stairs so gallantly. You are surprised at the soundness of your own constitution. Could it be your body is preparing itself for the rigours you have to face? For the trial ahead. Our hero is not going to crumble easily. Oh no, he's stronger than that. Adjust your hair, put on your hat. Old habits die hard.
VOICE:	Poor Joseph K feels seasick.
VOICE:	[*sung*] Imagining himself to be in a ship on heavy seas, with the waves roaring and breaking over him and he being pitched and tossed from one end of the ship to another, without ballast. Without guidance, a rudderless ship with the clients of the Court rising and falling, and being swept into the waves.
VOICE:	What would your father say about this, K?
K:	My father's dead.
VOICE:	Only to you, Joseph. Only to you.
FATHER:	[*as voice*] Joseph, Joseph, what have you done? *Joseph. Are you listening to me?*
K:	Father. Father. Is that you, father?
FATHER:	You know who it is. How can you sit there calmly with a criminal case around your neck?
K:	The calmer I am the better.
FATHER:	What is it you have done?
K:	I don't know. It's not the usual case in the usual criminal court.
FATHER:	That's bad.
K:	Why?
FATHER:	I mean it's bad. Things don't suddenly happen — you get indications. How pale you look. You should go home and rest. You're so weak. Build your strength up for the trial ahead of you.
K:	They probably wouldn't let me go anyway.
FATHER:	Who are they?

K: I wish I knew.

FATHER: Joseph, you've changed. Your brain's failing you.
          You'll lose the case if you act like this. Your indif-
          ference is driving me mad!

K: It's no use getting excited. It doesn't achieve
          anything. You know how much I respect what
          you say and I'll do anything I can to fight my
          case. But in my own way . . .

FATHER: If you're ready to really fight, then perhaps I can
          help you. First of all you need a lawyer. Go to
          Huld. He was at school with me. He's only a poor
          man's lawyer, but he's very good. Don't let us
          down. Goodbye Joseph. *Remember me . . .*

K: Goodbye father. In front of you, father, I lose all
          self-confidence and exchange it for an infinite
          sense of guilt.
          I begin to feel guilty already.
          But of what, I do
          Not know . . .

              [*The lights come up on stage and in audience.*]

              [K *finds himself alone — he walks off stage.*]

END OF ACT ONE

ACT TWO

Huld the Lawyer, or an Illustrated Account of the Law

Three enormous knocks are heard.

K: Open the door please.
[*The* TWO FIGURES *stand facing front — we see each person's point of view as in film.*]

LENI: Who are you?

K: The son of Mr K. He sent me to see Mr Huld.

LENI: Mr Huld is ill. It's eight o'clock. A very unusual time to call. [*miming her action*] Behind the grille in the door, two great dark eyes appeared. Then vanished again.

K: K assured himself that he had seen a pair of eyes — probably a new maid, afraid of strangers.

LENI: Once more the eyes appeared and now they seemed almost sad. They might be an illusion.

K: Please open the door. I've been recommended to Mr Huld.

HULD: Leni, who is it?

K: I am the son of your old friend Herman K. He sent me to see you.

HULD: Oh Herman! Come in, come in.
[*As* LENI *opens the door, using her arm as the door, the movement turns into a dance. The* CHORUS *leave screens and dance together until he arrives.* HULD *sits in a chair surrounded by* CHORUS *who become his clients and acolytes, and act out the information* HULD *imparts.*]
He doesn't come himself. He sends you. Well. Your father asked you to see how I am, eh? How nice of him — how very nice — well, why don't you ask me how I am?

K: How are you?

HULD: Don't ask. I'm terrible. Getting worse — difficult to breathe — can't sleep, and I'm losing my strength daily.

K: That's bad news.

LENI: You see. He's too ill to talk about business.

HULD: Aah! So it's not a sick visit — you came on business. It's all right, Leni. Has he come to see how I am?

CHORUS: *No.*

HULD: He only comes when he *needs* something. Well, that's how the world is. Leave us, Leni. Leni looks after me. She's a good girl.

LENI: Am I a good girl?

HULD: Of course you are.

LENI: And I have a doll-like rounded face?

HULD: With pale cheeks, and your chin quite round in its modelling.

LENI: Although I have somewhat protuberant eyes.

HULD: Not a jot. Not a jot.

K: *Would you please leave us.*

HULD: Go now, Leni. It's all right.

[LENI *moves into background watching.*]

To be quite frank with you, I know why you came. Your case is far too interesting to refuse to take on. *I accept the challenge.*

K: I don't understand. How could you know?

HULD: In my profession is it not natural I should have the ears of my colleagues? That cases would be discussed, and yours divulged — a word dropped here and there — a familiar sound, friends in the Court, a natter in the coffee shop, eh? Don't look round, but I have someone from the Courts visiting me at the moment.

K: Where? It's so gloomy in here — I can hardly see anything.

HULD: Shhh! Don't disturb him. He likes the dark. If only you knew how dreadfully overworked we are. Not so. The entire judiciary system needs to be overhauled. Your first plea must be ready for representation. That's very important, as the first plea often determines the whole case. Unfortunately, it is my duty as your lawyer to warn you that they don't always read the first plea. They simply file them away.

K: Why do they do that?

HULD: The observation and interrogation of the accused

are more important than pieces of paper. Besides which it gives the filing clerk something to do. They write down everything about you. Every minute of your daily life. Your most secret habits. Any bad ones?

CHORUS: *No.*

HULD: Good. Sometimes the sheer weight of written evidence accumulating day by day results in some confusion. An overworked ledger clerk, and the first plea is lost. They often lose the first plea and lose sight of the original intention. This makes counsel for the defence very difficult indeed. Remember they only tolerate the defence; strictly speaking, none of the magistrates on the Courts recognize counsel for the defence. This naturally has a humiliating effect on the whole profession.

K: The public would never tolerate that.

HULD: Proceedings are not public. They could be, but they're not. Only if the Law considers it necessary, which it doesn't.

K: But I still don't know of what I am accused.

HULD: Naturally not. The legal records of the case with charges are not available to counsel for the defence. Consequently, one doesn't know, with any precision, what charges to meet in the first plea. So you cannot draw up a plea just yet.

K: But how can I find out if they don't tell me?

HULD: Guess-work. You must guess from your interrogations. You have to sift the relevant details until a semblance of a charge emerges. Then one can draw up a convincing plea. So it's up to you. You must listen carefully — to each word — just that one word may give the clue to the whole affair. Don't worry. Things are not so hopeless as they seem. I have won outright cases that are even more desperate than this one. Perhaps less difficult. But hopeless. I have broken them down until they yielded the result to me. In my desk I have a stack of them. Unfortunately secrecy forbids me from disclosing them to you.

K: So you cannot know of what you are accused, or

HULD: who accuses you. The defence is not recognized by the judges, and you can't even see the charges. There is some difference of opinion on that. The Court considers the defence counsel merely as petty-fogging lawyers. Lawyers are abominably treated. Take a look at the lawyers' room next time you go back. Apart from the humanity which crushes itself in there, and with a window so small that if you want a breath of fresh air you have to stand on your colleague's shoulders, and even then you get the chimney smoke choking you and ending up with a black face. What about the hole in the floor? It's so big that a man's leg on stumbling can be seen jutting through the floor from the floor below. Complaints to even the authorities have not the slightest effect, and we can't even repair it.

K: Wouldn't it be better to write one's own defence, giving a short account of my life and the important decisions I had to make — I could explain why I made those decisions, and in retrospect comment whether I approve or disapprove? In this way the Court could judge whether I could be capable of some crime.

HULD: You need me, K. You need me.

[*He shits. The* CLIENTS *clear it up with a shovel and wipe his ass.*]

The most important thing is connections with officials in the Court. In that lies your chief value of defence.

K: But that's corruption. I must be judged on my alleged defence, whatever that is, not fail or succeed on the strength of your connections.

HULD: K, you will discover from experience that all grades of Court service with the exception of our friends here — have entwined into their organization venal and corrupt elements, whereby a breach has been made in the watertight system of justice. This is where your small lawyer tries to push in by bribery — listening to gossip and purloining of documents. These dirty methods may achieve momentary success, even lure more clients, but it has no effect on the furthering of the case — none!

Joseph K. Joseph K. You are so fortunate in your choice of lawyer. Only one or two lawyers have the same connections as me. Take a look around. The officials visit me of their own accord. Volunteering information, talking with great frankness. More! Sometimes letting themselves be persuaded to a new point of view. The secrecy of the system which although working against leakages, prevents the prosecution from actually prosecuting the case properly. They are too remote from the populace to understand their problems. They don't even see the people who they're prosecuting because they spend day and night and night and day trying to unravel the judicial system. The prosecution are in a constant state of agitation. That's why they come to me. Me. Huld — for advice. Now there's a story going round — what was it now?

[HULD *loses his train of thought. Meanwhile,* LENI *enters and takes* K's *hand — the* CHORUS *dissolve upstage.*]

LENI: I wanted to talk to you.

K: I wanted to talk to you too.

LENI: You mustn't bother him — think about me now for a change — I was afraid you wouldn't like me.

K: Like you? I couldn't keep my eyes off you.

LENI: I thought so too. Yet you kept me waiting. You'd better call me Leni.

K: I'd be glad to, Leni.

LENI: Do you really like me?

K: Like is not the word I would have chosen.

LENI: What word would you have chosen?

K: Well.

LENI: Go on, tell me, you brute. Say it, loudly to me, say it!

K: I'm a bit shy when you put it like that.

LENI: Don't be shy, Joseph. We'll be happy together. Don't be shy any more. You're brooding too much over your case.

K: Who told you that?

LENI: Don't ask me for names but I can give you some advice. Confess, Joseph, otherwise you won't get away from them.

HULD: Now I remember that story . . . now . . . damn, it's gone again.

LENI: I know a lot about what goes on in the Court. I could help you, you know.

K: Why is it I seem to recruit so many women helpers — first Miss Bürstner, then the Laundress and now her? I wonder what it is about me.

LENI: Have you a lover?

K: Yes and no. I have a photograph here.

LENI: [*looking at the photo*] I don't like her. She's rough and clumsy, but perhaps she's soft and kind to you. Small tough girls can't help being soft and kind. But would she be capable of sacrificing herself for you?

K: She's not that soft.

LENI: So she isn't your lover after all.

K: Oh yes!

LENI: Perhaps she is but you wouldn't miss her if you exchanged her for me?

K: Certainly I would.

LENI: [*seductive*] Would you really?

K: Yes.

LENI: You would?
         [*She gets closer and closer until kissing him.*]

K: Oh. You've kissed me!

CHORUS: K can feel her body against his breast and gazes at her rich dark hair. She clasps both hands round his neck, and kisses him on the back of his head. Yes . . . yes — she's biting him now, into the very hairs of his head. Hmmm. She gives out a bitter exciting odour like pepper. K puts his arms round her, and as she slides down onto the floor with a faint cry, utters . . .

HULD: Oh yes! I remember now. There was this official who flung lawyers down the stairs one after the other, so all the lawyers gathered on the landing and decided what they should do. They didn't wish to antagonize him — yet on the other hand their pleas had to be submitted . . . so they all agreed that the best thing was to tire the old man out. They ran up the stairs one after the other in relays, without a pause, and passively let themselves be thrown down the stairs into the arms of their colleagues. After an hour the old man couldn't resist any more. He was tired out. He was very tired, extremely tired. He died! The lawyers got in and submitted their pleas. That's what you might call legal strategy.

[*During his speech* HULD *and the* CHORUS *mime the story.*]

Leni!

[HULD *collapses back, stricken by a heart attack — the* CHORUS *attend him.*]

LENI: He's calling me. Here's the key of the door. Come back whenever you like. You belong to me now.

The Interrogators

Previous scene dissolves into the jury. Their faces appear to surround him, coming and going.

VOICE 1: Joseph. How could you do it? You've damaged your case quite badly which was beginning to go well.

K: Was it?

VOICE 2: Of course it was, but you hide yourself away with a filthy slut who's obviously the lawyer's mistress, and stay there for hours.

K: She was nice.

VOICE 3: Doesn't ever seek a pretext — conceals nothing, just runs off.

HULD: And there I sat — a man in my influence, who should have been won over.

VOICE 4: He makes no attempt — he's not fighting his trial.

K: I'm exhausted by my trial. I want to forget it.

HULD: He wants to forget what might in the end result in his own death.

VOICE 5: By negligence.

HULD:	Abusing me, Huld, a man of importance and influence who is actually in charge of the case at its present stage. There we sit trying to help you.
CLERK:	You were away so long there was no concealing it, but finally we couldn't ignore it.
HULD:	We were waiting for you, K.
VOICE 1:	And what do you gain by your behaviour? Nothing except a furtive moment of a cheap thrill.
K:	I gained something.
ALL:	Oh yes, what?
K:	I saw a painting of a judge.
ALL:	Oh, he saw a painting of a judge.
K:	He was seated on a high throne-like seat, in great dignity. He looked powerful, so wrathful that one felt that at any moment he might spring up with some violent gesture and pronounce sentence. He might be my Judge. I, the accused, could be standing on the lowest step leading up to the throne of justice. There was a great yellow carpet leading up the steps of the throne where he sat, very tall in his robe of justice.
VOICE:	He had himself painted like that. Actually he's a dwarf sitting on a kitchen chair, with a dirty old horse blanket doubled underneath him.

[*Laughter, which grows to a wild insanity.*]

K's Struggle with the Forces of the Filing Department

A FIGURE is left from previous scene — who starts the next one. All are involved with aspects of filing and clerical work.

CHORUS:	It's a winter morning. Snow was falling outside. K is in his office already exhausted in spite of the early hour.
	He left instructions nobody was to disturb him. He didn't want to be seen in this state . . . a face-saving operation.

Instead of working he twisted in his chair.

He sat motionless with bowed head.

The thought of his law-suit never left him now. He again considered whether or not it would be better to draw up a written defence and hand it to the Court.

The advantages of a written defence compared to a doubtful lawyer were obvious.

K had no idea what the lawyer was doing about the case.

Anyway, it didn't amount to much. It's been more than a month since Huld sent for him.

Not that Huld could do much anyway.

To begin with, he's hardly even cross-examined him.

K: There were so many questions to ask — to ask questions was surely the main thing. *I must shake off this lawyer. Send in petitions. Urge the officials daily to give their attention to it.* This won't be achieved by sitting meekly in the attics of the Court with your hat under the seat. I'll draft it in my lodgings at night. If the nights aren't long enough we'll go on shift work. The whole of my life will have to be written out. Every moment called to mind, down to the smallest action. Examine it in every detail. The Courts will encounter a man who stands up for his rights. And if I use the same energy I use in the Bank, there'll be no doubt about the outcome. And if we are to achieve anything we must banish from our minds absolutely the thought of my possible guilt. *There is no such guilt.*

[*Towards the end of the speech the* CHORUS *begin punctuating it with 'colon', 'full stop', 'exclamation mark', etc., as if they are taking a dictated letter.*]

If I conduct my own defence I will put myself entirely in the power of the Court. Will I have the strength to carry on? To put up a thorough-going defence . . . and this is the moment when I am supposed to work for the Bank. This is the time to interview clients, to try and make my life secure while my case is unfolding itself in the attics of

the Court, with officials poring over my charges.
And when the time comes for my work to be
judged will allowances be made for me? *Never* and
by nobody.

[*Blackout.*]

Huld!

Revisit to the Lawyer — and the Passing of Time

HULD: Progress has been made, K, but the nature of the
progress cannot be divulged, my dear boy.

[*Blackout — change positions.*]

The case has simply reached a stage and further
assistance ruled out in remote, inaccessible
Courts, where even the accused are beyond reach
of a judge.

[*Blackout — change positions.*]

So you came home and found on the table all the
pleas relating to your case returned to you. At
this stage, they're not relevant. It does not mean
the case is lost. By no means.

[*Blackout — change positions.*]

One must lie low. If you alter the disposition of
things you run the risk of losing your footing and
falling to destruction. Leave the lawyers to do
their work, K.

[*Blackout — change positions. Lights come up.* K *is on
top of* LENI.]

Leni. Are you still there? How do you like this
boy?

LENI: I hardly know him.

[*Blackout.*]

K dismisses Lawyer

NARRATOR: At long last K had made up his mind to take his
case out of his lawyer's hands. To screw himself
to this decision cost him a lot of energy. But he
was resolved.

Block

A strange little man leaps out of the darkness and on to K's back.

BLOCK:	Promise not to betray me.
K:	I'm not an informer.
BLOCK:	Perhaps I shouldn't tell you.
K:	You could risk it.
BLOCK:	I can?
K:	Yes.
BLOCK:	I'm the lawyer's only real client — I live here — I have a little room to myself.
K:	Is Leni your mistress?
BLOCK:	Oh God no! No! What are you thinking of?
K:	What's your name?
BLOCK:	Block. I'm a corn merchant. I'll tell you something, but to make sure we have a hold over each other, you must tell me one of your secrets.
K:	All right. If I do, will you get off my back?
BLOCK:	OK. [*He gets off slowly.*] I've been waiting for my case to come up for years, so I've taken on five lawyers apart from Huld.
K:	Five?
BLOCK:	And I'm negotiating for the sixth. You mustn't give me away.
K:	I said I wouldn't.
BLOCK:	He's vindictive, you see.
K:	Surely he won't harm you for having more than one lawyer?
BLOCK:	But it's not allowed, least of all back-alley lawyers, and that's what they are.
K:	Why do you need so many?
BLOCK:	I don't want to lose my case, you understand. I spent all my money on it. Sold my business which once filled the whole floor of a building. I attack it with all my strength, so I have no energy left for my other work. How can I? What do you think — could you? All the hanging about, keeping an eye on things, doesn't give much time for anything else. I have to be in the Courts nearly all the time. You know yourself what the air's like.

K: What do you do there?

BLOCK: Nothing. I simply wait. But what an effort that takes, sitting about. I saw you there the other day.

K: Saw me? What a coincidence. You were in the lobby when I passed through?

BLOCK: It's not such a coincidence. I'm there nearly every day. We knew you were an accused man. The accused are tired and distracted, and take refuge in superstition. The Bailiff said he saw on your lips the sign of your own guilt. [K *laughs nervously*.] Silly, isn't it?

K: On my lips? There's nothing peculiar about my lips, is there?

BLOCK: Of course not, but superstitious beliefs are a tradition and help the community combat the Law — gives them something to do.

K: Do what? It's so pointless — just hanging around waiting — They should form some community action.

BLOCK: Pointless. What do you know? You're a newcomer. You're young in the matter. You might think, as I once did, that you could safely wash your hands of the case, but you would be wrong. I can remember when my case was as young as yours. Like you I had just one lawyer. I collected evidence, attended every interrogation, made notes, submitted various petitions, showed my account books, ran backwards and forwards for bits of information. I had a detailed analysis of every case from ancient times that was supposed to resemble mine, and yet after all this, I couldn't detect one inch of progress.

K: What kind of progress did you expect to see?

BLOCK: A good question. I don't know. I'm a business man. I wanted to see palpable results, but the same old questions. The same answers. I complained to Huld — give me a date, I begged. Fix a day, for my trial . . . I'll call in other lawyers. I warn you . . .

HULD: [*As if in past.* HULD's *voice amplified.*] *Petty-fogging lawyers are useless. The slimy back-alley lawyers who sniff*

*around for the scraps. The lawyers in my circle are the great
lawyers. The great ones, Block, that accused men dream
about.*

BLOCK: That's untrue, absolutely untrue. Our lawyer
and his colleagues rank among the small lawyers.
The really great lawyers stand as high above
Huld as he does above the back-street cut-
throats, who are in turn that much higher than
your ordinary mercenary and thieving solicitors.

K: Who are these great lawyers? How does one get at
them?

BLOCK: I've no idea. I know of no instance when they
have intervened for an accused man. They take
on the clients they wish. Put it out of your mind.
Small lawyers seem so pale and insipid beside
them that you'd lose all faith. Unfortunately one
can't forget them, especially at night when the
thoughts start gnawing into your head.
[LENI *returns.*]

LENI: How close you've got. You're nearly bumping
heads.

BLOCK: He wants me to tell him about my case.

LENI: Go on then, tell him.

K: You were telling me about the petty-fogging
lawyers . . .

LENI: [*to* BLOCK] Go to him. He wants you.
[BLOCK *goes and takes* LENI's *place massaging*
HULD.]
Doesn't it strike you as surprising that the lawyer
will see you at any time you please? Without
notice . . . You take them for granted. I don't
want any thanks, only that you should be fond of
me.

K: But I am fond of you, Leni.

LENI: Then you're going to spend the night with me.
You're certainly going to do that, aren't you?
[*She drags him to the floor.* HULD *takes a screen,
placing it over* K *and* LENI, *creating an oblong
painting.*]

HULD: Leni has such a weakness for accused men. It's a
peculiarity of hers in finding nearly all accused
men attractive. She goes to bed with all of them,

and they all love her. I must make apologies to
you K, she even tells me about these affairs to
amuse me, which I allow. It doesn't surprise me
any more. If you have the right eye for these
things, you could well find accused men very
attractive. It's a remarkable phenomenon, for
being accused makes no obvious alteration in a
man's appearance, and yet there are those who
from a crowd of people can put their finger on the
accused. However, these men are not always
guilty. Therefore it must mean that merely being
charged invests one in that added attraction. Of
course there are some more attractive than
others. But they all are enhanced in some way.
Even that wretched creature Block.

[*He throws off* BLOCK.]

Leni, how do you like this boy?

LENI: I hardly know him.

HULD: Leni, don't take me for a bigger fool than I
already am. Bring me some tea.

[LENI *goes to* HULD. BLOCK *returns to* K, *jumps on his
back again.*]

K: Oh, why don't you go to bed?

BLOCK: K, you've forgotten your promise. You were
going to tell me one of your secrets.

K: All right. I'll tell you, but I want you to treat it
confidentially.

BLOCK: Of course, of course.

K: I'm not going to take on this lawyer. I'm going to
dismiss him.

BLOCK: [*Rushes around shouting.*] He's dismissing his lawyer. He's dismissing his lawyer.

[*Everyone begins yelling this.*]

[*Screens re-assemble as a bull ring with* CHORUS
standing on chairs watching over the top.]

K: I wish to select my own lawyer. It's my final
decision. I'm convinced that your efforts are not
enough. Now I am impatient. When I was alone
the case hardly bothered me, but since you represented me I've been waiting for something to
happen and it hasn't.

HULD: After a certain stage nothing new ever happens.
          How many clients have said exactly the same
          thing as you have! But yours isn't the usual case
          with the ordinary legal rights.

K: What's so different about mine?

HULD: In an ordinary case the lawyer leads his client by
          a slender thread, but in your case a lawyer must
          lift his client on his shoulders from the start, and
          carry him bodily without letting him down, until
          the verdict is reached, and even beyond it.

K: What steps do you propose to take if I retain you
          as my lawyer?

HULD: I shall continue with those measures that I have
          already begun.

K: I knew you'd come out with the same old plati-
          tudes. It's a waste of time to go on talking.

HULD: You've been treated too well. I'll show you how
          other accused men are treated, and perhaps
          you'll learn a thing or two. [*shouts*] Block.

          [VOICES *call* BLOCK *as if in court room.* BLOCK *enters
          very slowly, not daring to look up.*]

LENI: Block, the Lawyer wants you.

HULD: Is that Block?

          [BLOCK *falls back, shrivels as if from blow.*]

BLOCK: At your service.

HULD: What do you want? You've come at the wrong
          time.

BLOCK: Wasn't I called for?

HULD: You were, and as usual you still manage to arrive
          late.

BLOCK: Do you want me to go away?

HULD: Oh well, now that you're here, stay. Who is your
          lawyer, Block?

BLOCK: You are, Your Honour.

HULD: And besides me?

BLOCK: Oh, there is no one else besides you.

HULD: Are you sure, Block?

BLOCK: Oh yes. Absolutely sure.

HULD: Then pay no heed to anyone else.

BLOCK: Certainly, Dr Huld — I'm on my knees.

K: [*to* BLOCK] Why are you creeping on all fours?
          What's the matter with you?

BLOCK: Don't be so clever, for I am as clever as you are, and let me remind you of an old maxim: "People under suspicion are better moving than at rest *since they may be sitting on the balance without knowing it, being weighed together with their sins.*"

K: Don't you see? The Lawyer's trying to humiliate you.

BLOCK: Do you hear? Dr Huld — his case is five minutes old compared with mine, and he proceeds to give me advice.

HULD: Pay no heed to anyone.

BLOCK: Certainly . . . Dr Huld.

HULD: [*to* LENI] How's he been behaving himself?

LENI: He's been reading the papers you gave him.

HULD: Did he understand what he was reading?

LENI: He never got past the same page all day. It must be difficult for him.

HULD: [*as to a child*] Yes, the scriptures are difficult. He can see how difficult his case is, and how hard my struggle is for him. And who do I struggle for?

BLOCK: Why, it's ridiculous.

HULD: [*sings*] But it's for Block.

     [BLOCK *smiles sheepishly.* CHORUS *sing 'Block Block Block', etc.*]

HULD: Don't praise him. It makes it more difficult to tell him what the judge said today about his case.

BLOCK: [*trembling*] What did he say?

HULD: Not favourable.

BLOCK: Not favourable? [*Starts shaking.*]

HULD: Don't speak about Block, he said. But he's my client, I said. You're wasting your time, he said. I don't believe it. Block sincerely devotes himself to his case, even lives in my house to keep up with the proceedings. One doesn't often find such zeal. Admittedly he's repulsive, dirty, bad-mannered, loathsome, but as a client he's beyond reproach. "Beyond reproach?" he said. *What a lie!* Cunning, he replied, your client is cunning, but his ignorance is greater than his cunning. What do you think he would say if you told him that his case had not actually begun yet? That the bell marking the start of the proceedings had not yet rung?

[BLOCK *trembles and violently whimpers like a dog.*]
Quiet, Block. Don't get into a panic or if you do, I'll never tell you anything again. You should be ashamed to behave like that in front of my client, destroying his confidence in me. What's the matter with you? You're alive, aren't you? You're still under my protection. Your panic disgusts me. It's only a remark made by a judge who assumes that according to tradition a bell is rung to mark the opening of proceedings . . . *Block . . . stop pulling your hair out.*

[BLOCK *leaps at* HULD's *throat like a dog* — HULD *throws him off.* HULD *takes a stick and threatens* BLOCK — *makes him jump on a chair in his final humiliation so that he becomes a dog.* CHORUS *whistle and shriek in anticipation of this death of* BLOCK's *personality.*]

BLOCK: His case is only five minutes old compared to mine, and he already tries to give me advice.

[*Great noise is built up. As noise subsides only this* VOICE *is heard.*]

VOICE: Pay no heed. He's a finished man. He has no lawyer, no counsel, nobody to represent his case or defend him, or love him, or care for him, or tease or worry about, or go on walks with on Saturday after the Bank closes, or sit by the river with, or make his bed, or change his sheets, or wash out those understains, or argue with, or soothe, or mollify in the dark hours, or squeeze his fingers under the table, or smooth his brow, or lighten heavy days when nothing's been achieved. When nothing seems certain and an intervention could only be made with the encouraging nudge of a friend, which might just put the case back on the track. Nobody to make him a cake, or wait outside the Bank and be disturbed when he's late. Or take the stain out of his hat, or a grey thread from his hair, or brush the dust from his suit, or bite him on the ear or *welcome the police in when they come to arrest you for crimes so vile they dare not be named.*

[Bank staff appear frozen in an attitude which expresses their last reaction to the comments of the LAWYER.*]*

MANAGER: Not so, K. I feel a strong desire to help you. In your criminal case.

K: The Bank is where I work, not where I fight my case, not now . . . I have documents to discuss with important clients who wait upon my decision. What is this? A kind of torture sanctioned by the Court. Why don't you all leave me?

MANAGER: Go and see a man called Titorelli. He told me about your case. He earns his living as a court painter. He knows the judges. He could advise you. Don't see him here though . . . might make a bad impression.

K: Have I lost my powers of judgement already that I would invite a questionable character to the Bank in order to ask his advive, with the Manager's ears flapping just next door?

MANAGER: OK, K. Since you are forced to be away, you won't mind if somebody takes over your duties. After all, time is valuable.

K: Go ahead. Don't bother about me, you sly poacher. I can see what you're up to, but when my personal difficulties are over, I'll teach you to tread on my toes.

[The office backs away from his outburst, leaving TITORELLI *in frame as a painting.* K *pulls him out.]*

Titorelli

TITORELLI: Thank you very much. I got stuck inside a self portrait. That's very dangerous. Once I got stuck two days before someone came.

K: You're Titorelli the painter?

TITORELLI: That's right and you are Joseph K. I'm pleased to meet you.

K: How did you know?

TITORELLI: Word gets around. I have many friends. You've

been recommended to me? Very good. You come
to buy a painting, or have your portrait done?

K: Well yes, possibly.

TITORELLI: You like this, I'm working on just now?

This is a great judge.

This is a little judge's clerk.

Judge's secretary, very nice, not finished.

This one, bailiff of the Court.

Condemned man — a bit depressing, not for the
front room.

A guard of the Court, very strong, a little mad.

Court landlady, maybe you know her.

A bailiff, he like to be painted like a monkey, cos
his wife always make a monkey out of him.

This one's not for sale. She's like a Madonna.

Which one you take, two for the price of one.

> [TITORELLI *goes into picture frames. Series of positions.*]

You like dirty pictures? I make a quick portrait
for you. One sitting.

> [K *goes into frame.*]

It's beautiful, it's my best portrait. I hang it in the
gallery. Maybe I come in it with you . . . you like
that?

K: I can't see it.

TITORELLI: Take a look. [*They run out.*] You like it?

K: I didn't see it.

TITORELLI: You're not quick enough, put your skates on,
one, two, three, go.

> [*They race around.*]

K: Yes, it's very good.

TITORELLI: What are you talking about, there's no picture in
there. It's all right. I know why you come, you
flatter me. You pretend to buy my paintings,
when you really want to find out something about
the Court.

K: I do like your paintings.

TITORELLI: It's all right. You don't know how to tackle
me . . . Try to get round Titorelli. Don't worry.
Don't apologize. Take a seat; before I can help
you, I must know something about your case. Are
you innocent?

K: Yes.

TITORELLI: Between us, tell Titorelli.

K: Yes, I'm completely innocent.

TITORELLI: That's what they all say. They all say they're innocent. What have you done?

K: I've committed no crime.

TITORELLI: Don't be shy — something a little naughty, eh?

K: I've done nothing. That's the whole point.

TITORELLI: You're saying you're completely innocent. Then I will get you off all this myself.

K: The Court is firmly convinced of my guilt and can only be shaken from that position with great difficulty.

TITORELLI: Great difficulty! Never — if I were to paint all the judges in a row, masterpieces comparable to Greco, and you were to plead your case before all my paintings, you would have more success before the real Court than before my paintings.

K: You mean more success before your paintings than the real Court?

TITORELLI: That's very nice of you to say that, that too, but if you're innocent, I will help you.

K: Ah . . . It's to do with who you know.

TITORELLI: That's right. I know them all. I'm the court painter. You are born into the profession . . . It's an interesting position. Newcomers cannot grasp the intricacy of painting the judges like the old masters . . . My father was a court painter before me. His father was before him, his father before him, but the father before him was not a court painter.

K: What was he?

TITORELLI: He sells ice cream, because he couldn't paint. Gelato, choc-ice, tutti-frutti. [CHORUS *jump in and buy ice cream.*] I'm sold out. That was many years ago. And now his great grandson is a famous court painter. All right, what kind of acquittal do you want?

K: What do you advise?

TITORELLI: There are many kinds. But I tell you the first three. Acquittal definite, acquittal provisional, indefinite postponement, and a conviction which

is not an acquittal except from life, and that's
what we all want, but not just now.

K: Acquittal definite.

TITORELLI: Because you are innocent. It is the best one, but
that is only given if in your heart of hearts you
believe yourself to be innocent . . .

K: I am innocent, I am innocent . . .

TITORELLI: Unfortunately I must tell you, as far as I know, no
one has ever achieved acquittal definite.

K: But there must have been thousands of cases.
They can't all have been guilty. All the Court
needs is an executioner. Why have a trial at all?

TITORELLI: You are right. You're more than right. Acquittals
are never reported in the files since all the papers
are destroyed. So you have no proof of their existence in the files but legends have come down to
us. Some are so beautiful. I have painted many
pictures of them so we leave acquittal definite for
now.

K: Just for now.

TITORELLI: We come back to it later.

K: All right, tell me the other possibilities again.

TITORELLI: I make it simple for you. Acquittal provisional
requires great energy but for a short time. Indefinite postponement requires less energy but a
longer time. Make a choice. It lies with you.

K: Acquittal provisional.

TITORELLI: Very good. That's for you. I write down on a sheet
of paper an affidavit for your innocence. The text
of which has been handed down to me and is
unimpeachable. I say: I Titorelli believe Joseph K
to be innocent and guarantee his innocence. I go
from judge to judge collecting signatures. Some
judges don't believe me and want to meet you
personally. Then we go to the great judge in
charge of your trial.

    [*He goes to frame — impersonates the visit and the*
    GREAT JUDGE.]

He's not in, try again.

    [*Sound of dog barking.*]

I think someone is coming.

    [*They act out* TITORELLI's *vision.*]

JUDGE: What's the matter with you bothering me so late?

K: I come from Titorelli with an affidavit.

JUDGE: Ah, my good friend Titorelli. A friend of Titorelli is a friend of mine. I sign for you.

TITORELLI: Then you're free. Wonderful . . . but only provisionally free. The small judges that I know do not have the power to grant an acquittal definite. That is only given in the highest court, which is inaccessible to all of us.

K: What use is that?

TITORELLI: You're free to fight to the next stage of acquittal definite.

K: But you said nobody ever gets that.

TITORELLI: There's always a first time. With acquittal provisional the case is lifted off your shoulders. You're free to go to work. The papers continue to circulate, going from judge to judge, court to court, backwards and forwards with greater and smaller oscillations and permutations. No document is ever lost. Maybe five, maybe ten, maybe twenty years later you've forgotten about your case! You've forgotten that you ever had a case. I see you in the street in twenty years. "Who's that? Wait a moment, don't tell me. Ah, it's Mr K. Mr Provisional Acquittal, how's your case?"

K: What case? I have forgotten about my case.

TITORELLI: That's right. Then one day a judge's clerk picks up a piece of paper with your name written on it. It says Joseph K is only provisonally acquitted. The case is still valid. Arrest Joseph K and the case starts.

K: What use is that?

TITORELLI: You don't like that?

K: No.

TITORELLI: No. I don't like that either. It makes you always jumpy. I know what's for you — indefinite postponement prevents the case from going any further but you must be in daily contact with the judges. Greater diligence is needed. You daren't let the case out of your sight. Interrogations are frequent, but friendly at all costs. Invite the judges to tea. They're always trying to open up the case. Your case will go no further. But it will not be squashed, but not for you the sudden snatch in the middle of the night by the gnarled hand of the law saying: Joseph K. You are under arrest. Both these methods have this in common. They prevent the accused from coming up for conviction.

K: But they both prevent his definite acquittal.

TITORELLI: That's right. You've got it. So what do you like?

K: Nothing, your advice is useless!

TITORELLI: But my paintings are very good.

K: I don't want your paintings, I'd rather die!

TITORELLI: That can be arranged — you waste the time of Titorelli the greatest painter in the entire world — I'll show you what happens to the people who waste the time of Titorelli.

[TITORELLI *takes* K *and drags him behind a screen, painting* K *into a position of anguish and guilt.*]

[*The Court comes in, pushing* K *out of the screen — the picture frame is now full of masked faces who silently accuse him.*]

K's Trial

JUDGE: You're late! You should have been here one hour and five minutes ago.

K: Whether I am late or not, I am here now.

NARRATOR: K has only just arrived. The Court is packed. This is a popular case, which has drawn a great deal of attention. Indeed, the atmosphere, both in the Court and the air, is electric. The judges and prosecutors have just come in, after a short recess. The chief magistrate is searching for K's papers.

JUDGE: Well, you are a house painter I see.

K: No, I'm Chief Clerk in a large bank.

NARRATOR: The magistrate is now reading out the charges against him.

[*Their mouths open and shut —* K *hears silently the worst crimes he is capable of — we hear nothing —* K *collapses — the accusers leave — one man is left.*]

VOICE: *You will disappear as a dream and not be found, passing as*
        a vision in the night.

K: Upright men will be astonished at this and the
        innocent shall stir at the hypocrite.

VOICE: *Your bones, Joseph, are full of the sins of your youth, which*
        shall lie down with you in the dust.

K: The just shall hold on, and he that hath clean
        hands shall grow stronger.

VOICE: *You will suck the poison of asps. The viper's tongue will*
        slay you.

K: There is my hope and who shall see it?

VOICE: *The heavens shall reveal your iniquity and the earth rise up*
        against you.

K: [*as a roaring crescendo*] *Mark me and be astonished and lay*
        your hands on your own mouths. Wherefore do the wicked
        live? Wherefore do you see my ways and count my steps?
        I cry unto you, and thou dost hear me. I stand up and thou
        regardest me not, though they cry for my destruction. How be
        it you will not stretch your hand to the grave for me?

Bank Scene

The FIGURES *of the Court who remain on stage continue as*
office staff as if we have never left it — perhaps he has never
left the Bank.

ASST. MAN.: Are you all right, Joseph K?

K: [*unsure of exactly how or where he is*] Of course, why
             shouldn't I be? What are you doing, spying on
             me?

ASST. MAN.: You haven't forgotten, have you?

K: What?

ASST. MAN.: You have an assignment at the Cathedral this
             morning. You're to show one of our influential
             clients the sights.

K: Oh yes, you'd like me out of the way, wouldn't
             you?

ASST. MAN.: What do you mean?

K: I'm very dispensable nowadays. What are you
             trying to do? Get me out of the office to check my
             books?

ASST. MAN.:   But K. Since you are a member of the Society for the Preservation of Ancient Monuments, it seems natural that you should be his escort this morning. But if you'd rather not go.

K: All right, I'll go.

ASST. MAN.:   Don't forget your guide-book. Goodbye K.

[*He shakes* K's *hand rather warmly. The two hold hands for some while silently. It would appear that* K *was just about to say something. The* ASSISTANT MANAGER *appears to wait, hoping. For a moment it looks like two long lost friends about to say goodbye forever.*]

Leni

K *is walking towards the Cathedral. Music of church heard.* CHORUS *arrange the screens upstage — he walks through — * FIGURES *wait limply.*

LENI: I hate these wet murky days. Don't you, Joseph?

K: I don't have much time. I have to go to the Cathedral.

LENI: Why the Cathedral?

K: I'm showing one of our clients around the sights.

LENI: Oh Joseph, they're goading you.

K: *Pity I do not ask for any. Pity I do not expect, and pity is more than I can bear.*

[*She vanishes.*]

Yes, they're goading me.

Cathedral

FIGURES *outside the central aisle as gargoyles and angels.*

CHOIR: [*sung*] He's going in — but there is no one there to tell him it's empty except for an old woman kneeling before a Madonna.

K: Where the hell's my client?

CHOIR: You can wait half an hour.

That won't hurt you.

K: It's growing dark. So early in the day, too.
CHOIR: See the great pulpit
        Wrought all over with foliage, in which little
        angels were entangled, now vivacious, now
        serene.
K: I never knew this pulpit existed.
CHOIR: By chance K notices a verger in the shadows.
        He is watching him with the eyes of compassion.
        He is the guardian of us all.
K: What does he want, a tip?
            [VERGER *disappears.*]
CHOIR: Go now, Joseph. You'll never have a chance of
        going
        If you don't go now you cannot go
        During the sermon you'll have to stay as long
        As it lasts.
        Go now. Go now, Joseph.
            [PRIEST *is suddenly revealed as a giant effigy — screen
            folds back.* PRIEST *is stretched between a trapeze of rope
            — as a figure of Leonardo.*]
PRIEST: *Joseph K.*
            [*Singing continues in background.*]
        Joseph K. You are Joseph K?
K: Yes, I am Joseph K. I used to like giving my name.
        Nowadays it's a burden. Everybody seems to
        know it before they ask. The price of fame.
PRIEST: That's because you are an accused man.
K: So everybody keeps telling me. A bit early, isn't
        it, to preach a sermon? However, carry on, I'll
        listen. I'm supposed to show a client around the
        Cathedral. I'll hang around until the weather
        clears.
PRIEST: I'm here for you. I am the prison Chaplain, and
        you are the man I see. I had you summoned here
        to talk to you.
K: I didn't know that.
PRIEST: That doesn't matter now. What is that in your
        hand, K? A book of prayer?
K: No, an A to Z.
PRIEST: Put it away. You know your case is going badly?
K: Funny you should say that. I have done what I
        can. It's not over yet.

PRIEST: How do you think it will end?

K: It could turn out well, but I can't be sure.

PRIEST: I fear it will end badly. You are considered guilty. Your case won't get beyond the Lower Court. Your guilt is for the present supposed to have been proved.

K: But I'm not guilty. It's all been a big mistake. Everybody's guilty if I am, *including you.*

PRIEST: That's how the guilty speak.

K: So you're prejudiced against me too.

PRIEST: I have no prejudice against you, K. You are misinterpreting the facts. The verdict is not suddenly arrived at. The proceedings gradually merge into the verdict. What is your next move?

K: There are several possibilities I haven't explored yet.

PRIEST: You cast about too much for outside help, especially from women. It's not the right kind of help.

K: But women have great influence in the courts. The magistrates fall over backwards to get a sniff of them. Now if I could unite some women to join forces with me, I couldn't help but win through.

PRIEST: You don't know the nature of the courts, to speak like that. Can't you see one pace in front of you!

CHOIR: It was like an angry cry, but at the same time sounded
          Like the unwary shriek of one who sees another fall.

K: Since you're not preaching a sermon, why don't you come down from there?

PRIEST: I can't. I must speak to you from here. Otherwise, I might be swayed from my duty.

K: But you can spare a few moments.

PRIEST: As much as you need.

K: It's very good of you to say that. I'm sure I can trust you even if you do belong to the Court.

PRIEST: Don't delude yourself.

K: How am I being deluded?

PRIEST: You know in the writings that preface the Law your particular delusion is described?
          "Before the door stands a doorkeeper. Before this door stands the figure of a man waiting to gain

admittance to the Law. The doorkeeper says he cannot admit him just yet.

The man asks, "Will I gain admittance later?"

It is possible but not at this moment.

However, since the door gapes open as usual, the man ventures to peep inside.

"If you are tempted to try and enter without my permission but note that I am powerful . . . and I am only the lowest doorkeeper . . . through the hall is another door through which you must pass and another door through which you must pass and another yet and each man guarding them is successively stronger than I."

The man thinks the Law should be accessible to everyone but on reflection decides to wait . . . He waits for years . . . He is given a stool. He sits for years exchanging small talk, but never is allowed in. He eventually grows old and his eyes grow dim . . . He knows not whether his eyes are deceiving him, or whether the world is growing darker . . . Yet in all these years of waiting he has seen no other man seek admittance to the Law and questions the doorkeeper about this . . . He beckons the doorkeeper to him as he can no longer raise his body. The doorkeeper, seeing the man is near his end, says: "There could be no one else since the door was intended only for you. *I am now going to shut it* . . . "

K: The doorkeeper deceived the man, just as the Law is deceiving me. There is no door and no entrance.

PRIEST: But doesn't the keeper say, "The door was meant only for you"? There is no mention of deception in it. You must accept the Law's servant or doubt the Law itself. It is not necessary to accept everything as true, one must only accept it as necessary.

K: I want to go. Where is the main doorway?

PRIEST: Do you want to leave already?

K: Of course I do. I'm Chief Clerk at the Bank. I have work to do. *Preach to stone. What do you want from me?*

PRIEST: *Nothing. I only belong to the Court, you see who I am.*

K: *You are the prison Chaplain.*

PRIEST: *That means I belong to the Law. It receives you when you come and dismisses you when you go.*

K: *It's getting dark. Show me the way out.*

PRIEST: *Follow the wall. You'll come to the door.*

K: *Don't leave me. I can't find my way out of this darkness.*
[*Song of* CHOIR *grows.*]

[*A rope is stretched between* TWO MEN — *they change the shape and make stairs and endless corridors. As he arrives at the end of one stretch it reverses and he continues — the rope gets smaller until he is trapped in it.*]

VOICE: I must remain calm and analytical to the end. I always wanted to snatch at life with twenty hands. Was that wrong? Are they to say at the end of a year's trial I want to begin it again? I don't want that to be said . . .

K: Wait! There must be some arguments in my favour that have been overlooked. Wait! Where is my Judge? Whom I have never seen. *Where is the highest court, which I have never entered? Will someone help me? I hold out my hands. Like . . . a . . . dog.*

THE END

Steven Berkoff on *Metamorphosis*

So I came to Kafka on reading METAMORPHOSIS. I saw in him the most marvellous exertions of the imagination working inside the desperation of a strangled soul, this frightened human being — and thereby releasing its horrors. He touched me in all my chords of being from grotesque to simple, sublime humanity. No other writer quite manages this with the same power and insight. Kafka sees his contestants, or protagonists — but I call them contestants for the obvious overwhelming battles that they face.

The bug. Crushed, human Gregor — *Untermensch* — no better than the insect Kafka compares himself to in his letter to his father, when he accuses his father of hating him and despising his worth. So Kafka unrolls his scroll of agony over the minds of each generation as he did on mine, but in such a situation — oppressed bug, small, introverted, pathetic, inadequate, self-conscious — a parallel for a human being that one finds truly heroic. Gregor's struggles as an insect are indeed heroic. They are self-denying, they are overwhelming in the desperate struggle to overcome such a handicap, and are eventually death-giving. In the carapace of the insect he examines the family from this ground view. We see the frailty of human endeavour, greed and ambition — the protective sanctuary of the bourgeois family. Gregor as a bug is a hero of huge proportions: he snarls, he spits, leaps out of the family, meditates profoundly on the loss of human structure and emotions. A bug. Damned, filthy, loathsome thing in the back room. Introvert, artist, Jew, writer — therefore a bug. Berkoff, on reading this, could see in it the Theatre Of The Impossible, as Kafka's stories are the legends of the impossible. Who in the world has the resources, the higher flights of the absurdist imagination but the surreal magician, Berkoff — actor/writer/director/novelist and ex-menswear salesman from Stepney? He sets himself the task of keeping an audience awake by the brilliant attempts to plunge into the unconscious areas of the imagination. The vaults where dreams have stored their treasure trove. A man becomes an insect and his family reject, then tolerate, then loathe and then destroy, by neglect.

Jean-Louis Barrault's description of his struggle to create a horse in *As I lay Dying* gave me the confidence to plunge in. METAMORPHOSIS inspired as no play could, since it defies the convention of a play — which is a group of people screaming at each other and mouthing the neurotic obsessions of the writer.

But to act what is unreal, imagined, barely conceived — this is the province of the short story and the novel. How on earth can one stage that, The Theatre Of The Impossible?

The geometric shape of the insect governed my movements, for not only must one find the animal, but the animal *is* the *mise en scène*, the production. The insect must be seen, so should always be hovering, always watching the family. The ramp became his home and he must climb, so the set resembled a huge insect that he could climb (see stage directions). I, at one stage, had to climb out and hang from the ceiling like an insect — an interpolation of the story. So I practised in a gym and learnt how to climb and drop my body, hanging just by my legs and ankles, afraid nightly of being killed, but willing it, in my fanatic desire to outdo everyone else, my own self and my fears. The family, living in fear of time and money, sometimes became animated marionettes that moved, reflecting the insect's movements, so that they as a group, more than Gregor, were the dung beetle in reality. They were the creature, with their obsessive collecting of their balls of dung — their small, paltry, bourgeois achievements. Music underlined and scored the movement and in the end it was a piece of Total Theatre. In other words, it should engage the senses on all levels totally, as the senses are engaged in life, but with each discipline supporting the other — total theatre, total life, sound, movement, light, text, music.

METAMORPHOSIS never fails to move audiences whenever this adaptation is played.

METAMORPHOSIS

Metamorphosis was first performed at the Round House in London in July, 1969 with the following cast:

GREGOR	Steven Berkoff
MR. SAMSA	George Little
MRS. SAMSA	Jean James
GRETA	Petra Markham
LODGER	Chris Munke

Directed by Steven Berkoff

The play was subsequently performed by Steven Berkoff's London Theatre Group at the Hampstead Theatre Club in 1972, the Collegiate Theatre in 1976, and the Cottesloe Theatre and the New London Theatre in 1977; and directed by Steven Berkoff with the Nimrod Theatre Company in Sydney and the Haifa Theatre Company in Haifa in 1978, at the Mark Taper Forum in Los Angeles in 1982, at the Düsseldorf Playhouse in 1983 and at the Mermaid Theatre, London in 1986.

Mr Samsa attacking his son Gregor: "Apple for you, Gregor."

CHARACTERS

GREGOR   The Son
MR. SAMSA   Father
MRS. SAMSA   Mother
GRETA   Sister
CHIEF CLERK   Employer
THREE LODGERS (or one)

STAGE SETTING

A skeletal framework of steel scaffolding suggesting an abstract sculpture of a giant insect is stretched across the stage — this serves as the home of the family or carapace. The stage is void of all props — everything is mimed — apart from three black stools (metal) situated equidistant downstage for the family to use. The scaffolding narrows at the back, containing in its centre Gregor's room or cage. He is on a small ramp (2' 6") suggesting always that Gregor is hovering above the family. He is always watching — forever aware. The living quarters that the family use are demarcated by sharply lit areas, thus when Greta opens Gregor's door a hard light snaps down on the cage indicating the family can now see him. When this light is off the door is shut — that is stage reality for the family — the second reality for the audience is, of course, that he is always seen in half light but his family cannot see him. Within his cage are horizontal metal bars allowing Gregor to crawl gradually up the wall. At the top of the cage the bars fan out to the edge of the scaffolding downstage to enable Gregor at a later point of the play to climb along the ceiling upside down and beetle-like.

Since Gregor's beetle metamorphosis is an attitude deliberately taken to expressively show his inner-state, his naked dehumanized personality, a struggling insect, I chose to adapt/direct the play as formally as possible, suggesting the family's joy/anguish very often in fixed attitudes — choreographed reactions — Victorian gestures, frozen movement reminiscent of old prints. The movement becomes an analogue to the hard, bright, mechanical insect movement of Gregor — they might be separate units of the beetle themselves. This style, rather than diminishing the impact of the story by reducing naturalistic stage activity, did for many have an even more powerful effect, as if the memory of events and of people is retained in the mind's eye almost as stills — sometimes slightly blurred and out of focus. Perhaps this is why 'old photographs' strike so powerfully chords of association.

The FAMILY *enters one at a time — backcloth lit — figures appear in silhouette. Each one enters in the character he or she is going to play, and performs a small mime condensing the personality into a few seconds.* MOTHER *is first — describes a sad face — leaves a pained heart and angst.* FATHER *next strolls boldly on in boots and costume of mid-European lower middle-class tradesman — trousers in socks — braces — no jacket, looking like Hindenburg. Then* GRETA, *as student with violin. Then* GREGOR, *who just walks on and smiles — an amiable being.*

As each speaks they form a line behind each other. On the last line they take on the movement of an insect by moving their arms to a particular rhythm. As no front lighting is used, this has the effect of an insect's leg movements.

MR. S: [*enters*] As Gregor Samsa awoke one morning from uneasy dreams . . .

MRS. S: [*enters*] He found himself transformed in his bed into a gigantic insect . . .

GRETA: [*enters*] His numerous legs, which were pitifully thin compared to the rest of his bulk, waved helplessly before him.

[*Movement starts.* GREGOR *is in front. Suddenly the movement stops —* FAMILY *dissolve the beetle image by moving away — leaving* GREGOR *still moving as part of the insect image.*]

[*Front lights come up revealing* FAMILY.]

GREGOR: What has happened to me?

FAMILY: He thought.

GREGOR: It was no dream.

GRETA: [*as clock*] He looked at the alarm clock ticking on the chest.

GREGOR: Half past six and the hands were quietly moving on.

MRS. S: Gregor, Gregor?

MR. S: Said a voice.

GREGOR: That gentle voice . . .

GRETA: It was his mother's . . .

MR. S: His mother's . . .

MRS. S: His mother's . . .

[*Fade.*]

[*Slow Tick*]

[*Lights snap up on the centre area downstage revealing* GREGOR *standing behind* GRETA — *scenes of pre-insect life. Each speak their own thoughts which run contrapuntally.*]

GREGOR: [*indicates*] I'm Gregor Samsa — there's my sister Greta.

GRETA: [*motionless*] There's brother Gregor.

GREGOR: Isn't that nice that she waits for me.

GRETA: I always wait up for him.

GREGOR: Glass of milk on the table then bed — up again at four a.m. Yes, four a.m.! To catch the five a.m. train.

GRETA: He doesn't come home often.

GREGOR: Daily! What a life — what an exhausting job, and I picked it.

GRETA: He works so hard.

GREGOR: I picked it? I'm a commercial traveller in the cloth trade — I have to work to keep them.

[*Lights snap on downstage left and right revealing* MOTHER *and* FATHER *both frozen.*]

GRETA: But he also makes things at home.

GREGOR: Who else can do it? Father's ill so they rely on me totally.

GRETA: He recently made a picture frame and in it he put a picture cut out of an illustrated magazine.

GREGOR: On my back it rests — their fortunes rest on my back like a great weight.

GRETA: It shows a lady with a fur cap and fur stole sitting upright and holding out to the spectator a huge fur muff into which the whole of her forearm had vanished.

[*Image of above — music.*]

GREGOR: The warehouse was better — one didn't have to worry about the travelling.

GRETA: It was very good.

GREGOR: I feel sick.

[*Dissolve.*]

[*A loud ticking is heard which continues throughout the next scene —* GREGOR *marches behind his* FAMILY *who in time to the ticking call out* GREGOR's *meaning for them. Double time for* GREGOR *going about his work.*]

GRETA: Gregor!

MR. S: Cash!

GRETA: Gregor!

MR. S: Shoes!

GRETA: Gregor!

MR. S: Cigars!

GRETA: Gregor!

MRS. S: Food!

GRETA: Gregor!

MR. S: Beer!

GRETA: Gregor!

MRS. S: Clothes!

[*As* GREGOR *comes to stop behind* GRETA — FAMILY *mime actions of domestic life in time to ticking resembling those automatic figures in wax-works — they repeat same combinations of gestures — only when they speak do they freeze the movement.*]

GRETA: Milk, Gregor?

[*Image — actors as marionettes.* FATHER *smokes cigar and drinks.* MOTHER *sews.* GRETA *reads her school books.*]

GREGOR: Thanks — you're up late, why aren't you in bed?

GRETA: I thought I'd wait up for you. What's the matter?

GREGOR: My back's aching — must be carrying these samples all day.

[*Freeze action during next five speeches.*]

MR. S: Did you sell much?

GREGOR: Not as much as last week.

MR. S: [*disappointed*] Oh! — never mind — it'll be better tomorrow.

GREGOR: Perhaps.

MR. S: Of course it will.

[*Continue action.*]

GREGOR: Ssh . . . listen . . .

GRETA: What?

GREGOR: It's raining again — hear it beating on the window gutter?

MRS. S: [*listening*] It's been raining for ages.

GREGOR: Oh God! [*Sits down wearily.*]

GRETA: What is it?

GREGOR: I'm so exhausted.

MR. S: Go to bed then.

GREGOR: Always tired — travelling day in, day out.
            [*Image — the feet of the* FAMILY *race while they sit —
            faces reveal the agony of* GREGOR's *life — they become
            chorus for his statements.*]
            On top of worrying about train connections —
            snatching odd meals, (and if I arrive late at some
            small town, trudging the streets looking for an
            hotel). [*Repeat this sentence twice, once fast, once slow.*]
MRS. S: I thought you preferred it to the warehouse.
GREGOR: Not any more — a man needs his sleep.
GRETA: Well, go to bed then.
GREGOR: [*ignoring her*] The other travellers have it easy —
            they're still at breakfast when I've returned with
            the morning's orders.
            [*Image of above — music.*]
            Sometimes it's still dark out when I leave and the
            mornings are so empty and bitterly cold . . . I
            think that's why I've got a stiff back.
GRETA: Why don't you leave?
GREGOR: I will one day — rest assured, as soon as I've paid
            off father's debt to him, I'll go right up to the
            chief himself and tell him what I think of him.
GRETA: [*giggling*] Oh that would be fun — imagine his
            face.
            [*Image —* FATHER's *image of* CHIEF CLERK.]
GREGOR: It would knock him sideways if I did that . . .
            [*Image of* CLERK — *tilting sideways.*]
            He's such a strange little man . . . he's got an irri-
            tating habit of sitting high at his desk and talking
            down to me — and I have to crane my neck
            because he's hard of hearing.
GRETA: Is there much to pay off?
GREGOR: It should take another five years.
MRS. S: Oh! As long as that!
GREGOR: Then I'll cut myself loose!
GRETA: Good, and if you're lucky it might be sooner.
GREGOR: And that's another thing — you're always
            making casual acquaintances.
            [*Image of* FAMILY *going to meet and then parting, never
            quite succeeding in the act — music.*]
            And before you've time to become friends you're
            off again. [*Moves his joints in time to ticking . . . first*

intimations of insect state.] I don't know what's happening to me — all my joints feel stiff.

GRETA: Perhaps you shouldn't go in tomorrow — don't go in — I'll get a doctor for you in the morning.

MR. S: }
MRS. S: } NO!

GRETA: Why not?

MR. S: It would look suspicious.

GREGOR: I've not had a day's illness in five years.

MR. S: The Chief Clerk himself would come here with the insurance doctor and put it all down to laziness.

GREGOR: I mean I feel quite well really so they wouldn't be wrong, would they?

GRETA: But you look so tired and pale.

MR. S: That's the penalty for being a good salesman.

FAMILY: *Oh Gregor, you're so good to us!*

MR. S: You go to bed now.

GRETA: And have a good night's sleep.

MRS. S: And I'll make you a lovely breakfast in the morning.

GREGOR: I could sleep for ever. [*Moves slowly back to cage.*] Goodnight, Greta. [*Collapses into cage which is unlit — he is on his back motionless.*]

FAMILY: [*in harmony*] Goodnight, Gregor.
　　　　[*Blackout.*]

[*Fast ticking starts — day begins. A hard light snaps on downstage — everything works by the clock — movements again are purely functional, speech patterns are geared to movement and ticking.*]

[*Cyclorama lit in white — FAMILY in three white spots. GREGOR a black silhouette, feet up — arm moving in and out.*]

[*Image — FAMILY at breakfast, GREGOR on his back, the still stiff insect before waking.*]

[*The mime of FAMILY eating, looking up, wondering where GREGOR is, in unison linked as a chorus.*]

MR. S: It's half past six. Where's Gregor?

MRS. S: Half past six — Oh dear — perhaps the alarm clock's not gone off.

MR. S: Did you set it?

GRETA: Set it? Yes. I set it for four o'clock.

MR. S: }
MRS. S: }   Four o'clock.

GRETA: I set it properly.

MR. S: That ear-splitting noise should have woken him.
            [*They move back on stools.*]

MRS. S: Gregor? [*sung*] Oh, Gregor! It's quarter to seven
            already — shouldn't you have been at work?

GREGOR: Yes — yes — thank you, Mother — I'm getting up
            now.

            [*The ticking stops suddenly — the silence accentuates
            the stillness — their world of eating and normality
            ceases. They move now in very slow motion beginning to
            show anguish.*]

            [*Image — FAMILY silently mouth their concern. They
            hold gestures in listening.*]

            What's happened to me — everything seems the
            same — it's still raining outside — Oh, my leg —
            what's wrong with my legs? Turn over and go
            back to sleep, it's a bad dream — I can't turn over
            — I can't turn!

            [*FAMILY turn on stools complete circles rather than
            walking up to his area. The stools are metal with shiny
            tops.*]

FAMILY: Gregor!

GREGOR: Shut my eyes — I'm dreaming. [*to his legs and arms
            as if wishing them to dissolve*] Go away! It's nonsense
            — it must go away — spots on my belly? Ooh!
            They're itching. [*Scratches furiously.*] Must sleep —
            but I can't sleep on my back!

            [*FAMILY turn other way on stools — their faces return
            showing anxiety — 'Never has he been late before' —
            expression of dismay, fear, wonderment.*]

FAMILY: Gregor!

            [*Interjections become more frequent from FAMILY.*]

GREGOR: I have to work — it's quarter to seven — why
            didn't I hear the alarm — the next train goes at
            seven and my samples are not even packed and
            even if I caught the train there'd be a row — I
            knew I was sick yesterday.

[FAMILY *turn different directions on stools like computer wheels.*]

GRETA: Gregor — aren't you feeling well? Are you needing something?

GREGOR: I'm just ready — won't be a minute.

GRETA: Open the door, Gregor — please do.

GREGOR: Yes, soon — soon.

[*Very loud knock on door, the* FAMILY *rise.*]

[*Three loud knocks followed by the* CHIEF CLERK *who makes a long entrance while the* FAMILY *speak — sharing the next speech.*]

[*Image — they repeat this speech once still, once in panic — figure of eight round stools.*]

MR. S: Oh dear — that's bound to be somebody from the warehouse/

GRETA: The porter would have reported his failure to turn up/

MRS. S: That porter was the boss's boot-licker, spineless and stupid/it's sure to be him . . .

CLERK: [*enters*] No, Mr. Samsa, it's the Chief Clerk.

[FAMILY *all sit in shock.*]

Young Mr. Samsa's not been in this morning —
[CHIEF CLERK *doffs imaginary hat — he walks along the line of the* FAMILY *to* MRS. S. *from stage L to R.*]
Ah, Mrs. Samsa, good morning — thought I'd drop round, see what the trouble is.

[*Pause — silence as they turn to face* CHIEF CLERK.]

GREGOR: [*slow*] Snoop . . . Chief Clerk himself.

[CHIEF CLERK *wears steel-tipped tap shoes so he can tap the floor like an impatient clock — he taps the floor until* MRS. S *says* 'I'm terribly sorry' *since there is a pause that allows that impatience.*]

MRS. S: I'm terribly sorry, but our son's not feeling well — I don't quite know what's wrong — it's very unlike him — he's very conscientious as you know — thinks of nothing but his work.

[CHIEF CLERK *moves menacingly in from L. They turn slowly. The* FAMILY *shrink back on their chairs — freeze in attitudes of fear and oppression by authority represented by the* CHIEF CLERK.]

CLERK: Hmmm!

	[Image — FAMILY threatened by CHIEF CLERK.]
GREGOR:	What a villain — it is impossible to be a couple of hours late without sending the Chief Clerk himself to investigate — giving my family something fresh to worry about, it'll soon go away — like those little pains I had, caused by awkward postures which soon disappeared when I woke up. *[Starts rocking.]* Mustn't hit my head . . . mustn't lose consciousness now.

[CHIEF CLERK moves now to stage L in front of and round stool and now oppresses MR. SAMSA.]

MRS. S:	Gregor! The Chief Clerk's here!
GRETA:	He's worried.
MR. S:	Why you are not at work.

[CHIEF CLERK is now on stage L. FAMILY shrink in opposite position and freeze.]

GREGOR:	I know, I know. I only want to get up quietly without disturbing anyone, put my clothes on, and have my breakfast. *[GREGOR, who has been on his back the whole time, now attempts to shift to his front.]* Must push — push — harder — Harder. *[Thumps over completely on his front.]*

[FAMILY sit bolt upright after crash.]

CLERK:	Sounds like someone fell in the next room.

[MR. and MRS. SAMSA thread these next speeches inside each other, MR. SAMSA walking up and down stage with GRETA punctuating the odd 'Gregor'. Whilst downstage MRS. SAMSA attempts to smooth the CHIEF CLERK's fears. This is the first time the FAMILY actually move to his room area. Movements are steady. Symmetrical, beating, harmonious patterns — not yet driven into confusion, more concerned.]

[Image — ordered confusion as they walk to cage and CHIEF CLERK eats GREGOR's breakfast.]

[MR. SAMSA and GRETA move to GREGOR's area. A synonymous pattern emerges — they freeze on the point of impact, on the end of MRS. SAMSA's speech — a split second pause — a picture — frozen — of concern.]

MR. S:	Excuse me. *[Goes to GREGOR's room.]* Gregor — the Chief Clerk himself has come down to see you.
GRETA:	Gregor.

MRS. S: He's not really well, believe me. [*Freeze.*]

MR. S: Wants to know why you didn't go in today.

MRS. S: What else would make him miss the train? [*Freeze.*]

MR. S: We don't know what to say to him.

GRETA: Gregor.

MRS. S: He thinks of nothing but his work. [*Freeze.*]

GRETA: Gregor.

MR. S: Besides, he wants to talk to you privately.

GRETA: Gregor.

MRS. S: It makes me almost cross the way he never goes out in the evenings. [*Freeze.*]

GRETA: Gregor.

MR. S: So please open the door.

MRS. S: Dancing and things like that.

MR. S: He won't mind if your room's untidy.

MRS. S: He just sits reading or studying the railway time-tables. [*Freeze.*]

GRETA: [*to* GREGOR] Please Gregor — you'll get in trouble.

MRS. S: [*to* CLERK] The only amusement he gets is doing fretwork — do you know he spent three evenings cutting out a lovely picture frame — he's very clever with his hands ... I'm sure he's unwell ... it's not like him.

CLERK: I can't think of any other explanation, madam — and while I hope it's not serious, I must say that in business one must ignore slight indispositions — work must go on.

MRS. S: Oh yes, I absolutely agree — well I hope it's not slight ... [*One movement reaction from* FAMILY *amplifying her statement.*] I mean not serious ... [*Repeat.*] ...[*Breaks off not knowing what to say.*] Oh, I don't know.

MR. S: [*knocking at door*] Gregor. Once and for all. Will you let the Chief Clerk in?

GREGOR: Leave me in peace!

    [*There is a shocked silence.* MR. SAMSA *moves away in gesture of bewilderment, fear, puzzlement as the* CHIEF CLERK *comes to take his place at the door.*]

    [FAMILY *listen frozen/intent.*]

CLERK: [*trying door*] Mr. Samsa — what is the matter with
           you — why have you barricaded yourself in your
           room, just answering yes and no all the time —
           causing your good parents a great deal of trouble
           and neglecting your business duties in an incred-
           ible fashion? [*Silence.*] You amaze me — you really
           amaze me — I always thought you quiet and
           dependable and now you seem bent on making a
           disgraceful exhibition of yourself. The Chief did
           hint that a possible explanation for your disap-
           pearance was the funds that you were entrusted
           with.

               [*Image* — FAMILY *outrage and opposition.*]

FAMILY: Oh no!

CLERK: I, of course, defended you, but seeing your behav-
           iour now makes me doubt the wisdom of my
           actions!

MR. S: He's an honest boy!

MRS. S: He'd never do that!

GRETA: Never! Oh Gregor, open the door please.

               [*They incline heads in — no response — move down-
               stage slowly and thoughtfully.*]

               [*Image — what to do? Hands flapping behind backs.*]

               [CHIEF CLERK *moves downstage — even his authority
               has failed.* GRETA *rushes to* FATHER — *who pats her
               encouragingly as she starts to cry.* CHIEF CLERK *and*
               MOTHER *look at* MR. SAMSA, *who expresses helpless-
               ness.*]

CLERK: Do you have another key?

GRETA: Another key — I don't think so.

MRS. S: We've never needed more than one key before.

CLERK: Does he always lock himself in?

               [*They search for key.*]

MRS. S: He never used to — it's a habit he got into
           through travelling in strange hotels — he said
           that you should always lock the door at night —
           he's very prudent like that.

CLERK: [*getting exasperated*] I intended to discuss this with
           him in private but as he's wasted my time I don't
           see why I should . . . for some time past his work
           at the firm has not come up to scratch, Mr.
           Samsa, and this can't go on much longer.

GREGOR: [*Crying out — a guttural voice — a creature less than a human — his words become less and less distinguishable to them. They all rush to the door.*] Sir, I'm just going to open the door — this very minute . . . slight illness — an attack of giddiness — kept me in my bed — getting up now — just a moment longer — sudden attack — be as right as rain soon — no foundations in your reports — no-one said anything to me — obviously you haven't looked at my last order — spare my parents — I'll catch the eight o'clock train — Don't let me detain you — please make my excuses to the Chief.

    [*Image — total* FAMILY *confusion — figures twist and whirl around each other like a frenetic dance.*]

CLERK: [*Rushing downstage —* FAMILY'*s movement becomes faster and faster as confusion breaks loose.*] Did you make out a word of it — is he trying to make fools of us?

MRS. S: [*moving downstage with* GRETA] Oh dear, perhaps he's terribly ill and we're tormenting him.

MR. S: My son has never behaved like this.

CLERK: No respect.

MRS. S: Greta!

GRETA: Yes Mother.

MRS. S: Gregor is ill — go for a doctor.

MR. S: My son — open the door.

CLERK: The man's mad.

MRS. S: Go quickly.

MR. S: My son!

MRS. S: [*to* CHIEF CLERK] Did you hear how he was speaking?

CLERK: It was almost inhuman!

MR. S: And get a locksmith, Greta — quick as you can!

MRS. S: I'll boil a kettle.

    [*Image —* FAMILY *frozen in anguish mixed with determination.*]

    [*Image on A, B, and C.*]

GREGOR: [*from cage — witnessing scene*] Why were they so upset — *A*. Because I wouldn't get up and let the Chief Clerk in. *B*. Because I was in danger of losing my job? *C*. Because the Chief would start nagging my parents for money again. Surely these were things one needn't worry about now . . . [*As if to* FAMILY *now through door — there are times in the beginning when* GREGOR *speaks his thoughts aloud and times when he attempts to communicate directly with the* FAMILY. *With slight emphasis in light change and vocal manner these two states are not confused.*] I'm not really well . . .

MR. S: [*downstage, comes to life*] You see, he's not well, otherwise he wouldn't be lying in there.

[*More noises from room.*]

MRS. S: Ssh! He's turning the key . . . Ssh!

[*All listen intently to every sound the key makes — all making sounds of encouragement. It takes* GREGOR *a painfully long time to unlock the door.*]

GRETA: [*cries out*] Good, Gregor! Good!

MRS. S: Ssshhh!

[*Action freezes at the door.*]

MR. S: [*moves downstage*] What confusion, was his absence such a crime, that no less a person than the Chief Clerk could investigate it?

[*Image —* FAMILY *face downstage reversing the scene, i.e., audience see their faces, fear, anger from* GREGOR*'s point of view.*]

MRS. S: [*moves downstage*] What a fate, to work for employers where the slightest failing causes the greatest suspicion.

GRETA: He's probably more tormented than all of us!

CLERK: He need only open the door to put an end to all suspicion.

MRS. S: Gregor, open the door.

MR. S: Come on — open up.

CLERK: Samsa!

GRETA: Come on, Gregor, hold on to the key.

GREGOR: With what, my jaw? I have no teeth.

[*Silent mime shouting.*]

GRETA: Encourage him, don't threaten!

MR. S: Gregooor!

MRS. S: Open the door.

[*Image — creature in panic spinning around his cage.*]

FAMILY: [*shout*] Gregor.

[GREGOR *retreats to the back of the cage.*]

[*Image — lights go out on stage except cage area (in dark they return to cage area). We hear the knocking from beetle's point of view — amplified, loud, threatening. As stage lights come on — it suggests door has opened — there is a moment of total stillness such as can only exist in a nightmare. More still than a painting — They reflect his movements as he descends.*]

GREGOR: Nearly there — now pull down again.

[*Another loud click — door opens — indicated by a strong light which comes up on his area.*]

FAMILY: [*with a sigh of relief*] Aaaaah!

[*They see him for the first time. Stand back — gasp. Slowly come down — lights come down and throw his beetle silhouette against the backcloth — the whole structure becomes an ugly beetle shape with long moving shadows . . . The* FAMILY *retreat slowly — their bodies reflecting the horror they have seen — all movements become slow until lights normalize . . .* GREGOR *slides down his rostrum like a jelly oozing into the room — he moves as one mass.*]

GREGOR: [*While speaking the* FAMILY *move away inch by inch.*] I'll put my clothes on at once — pack my samples and be off — I want to work you see — travelling is a hard life but I couldn't live without it. I'm in great difficulties but I'll get out of them — travellers are not popular, sir . . . people think they earn stacks of money and have a good time, you know that's not true — it's just because they're never seen in the office, they're always working — don't let the Chief's judgement be swayed against me, sir — don't go away without a word to me to show that you think me in the right, at least to some extent.

[CHIEF CLERK *screams and exits. The sound of* CHIEF CLERK*'s scream brings* FAMILY *back to life.*]

MRS. S: Help! For God's sake, help!

MR. S: Shoo! Get back. [*Motions with stick.*] Get back! Get back! [*Continues hissing, raises stick like spear.*]

GRETA: Don't, Father! You're confusing him.

MR. S: [*continues hissing*] Quiet! Stay with your mother! Go on — back you go! [*Using stick drives* GREGOR *back to room.*]

GREGOR: Gregor was quite unpractised in walking back-
            wards and he was afraid of annoying his father
            even further by the slowness of such a rotation.
            [*Image — MR.* SAMSA *takes a bamboo cane (symbol-
            izing his stick) 5 metres — and impales insect on it. It
            catches* GREGOR *in his soft belly and he is tipped
            backwards into his cage.* GREGOR *shrieks in pain as if
            he had been penetrated.*]

MR. S: His father for his part had no intention of making
            things easier by opening the door — but never-
            theless wanted him out of the room as soon as
            possible.

GRETA: Gently Father, don't hurt him.
            [GREGOR *crawls into his room. They all breathe a sigh
            of relief and collapse into each other's arms. The back-
            light makes them tormented silhouettes acting out*
            GREGOR's *agony as the* FAMILY *together take on*
            GREGOR's *shape.*]

            [*Image — the* FAMILY *are now symbolizing* GREGOR
            and enact the injuries inflicted on the beetle's body.]

MR. S: Oh, God!
            [*They move behind each other, arms stretch in sup-
            plication — at the same time they as a chorus reflect*
            GREGOR.]

            Oh, God!
            [GREGOR *unseen, masked by* FAMILY.]

GREGOR: Crushed by body returning to my room [*slow*].
            Flanks bruised [*quick*]. Blotches stain the floor.

FAMILY: Oh, God!

GREGOR: I've damaged my leg — will it heal?
            [FAMILY *again as creature.*]
            Will it heal?

MR. S: [*destroying image*] Don't let the neighbours see —
            lock the doors — draw the curtains.
            [*Images — doors/curtains through the body and arms.*]

GREGOR: And I wounded my jaw when I opened the door.
            [FAMILY *recreate this.*] I know I damaged it because
            a brown fluid came out of my mouth. Dripped
            over the key and on to the floor.
            [*Dissolve jaw image — suddenly aware of the* CHIEF
            CLERK's *exit.*]

MR. S: The Chief Clerk!

[*They move downstage to stools.*]

He must be soothed, detained, won over, the whole future of the family and Gregor depends on it.

MRS. S: He mustn't return to the warehouse in that frame of mind.

MR. S: Follow him, he's partial to ladies and will be guided by you.

[*They are crouched behind their stools as if watching him in the distance.*]

[*Image — the frantic eyes and outstretched hands following him.*]

MRS. S: [*pointing*] He's already down the stairs.

MR. S: He's in the street!

GRETA: He takes one last look backward.

FAMILY: He's gone.

[*They fade out as* GREGOR *speaks from cage.*]

GREGOR: I can just imagine the story the Chief Clerk will tell my colleagues — how their ears will prick up — they'll draw lots to see who takes over my area [*moans*]. Isn't it curious how one plucks shreds of comfort even from disaster — the fact that I was now the centre of attention gave me no small tinge of pleasure.

Next Scene — Evening

Lights come up downstage . . . FAMILY *in last positions.*

MRS. S: For a few moments that morning I thought I was dreaming but the dream stayed.

GREGOR: What a quiet life our family has been leading, and as he sat there motionless, staring into the darkness, he felt great pride he'd been able to provide for his parents and sister in such a fine flat.

GRETA: They'll think Gregor's deserted them, they'll worry.

[*Live scratch.*]

GREGOR: But what if all the quiet, the comfort, the contentment were to end in horror?

MR. S: If only we could have sat down quietly and worked out a solution — the Chief Clerk created the panic.

GREGOR: I must keep moving, crawl up and down my room.

MR. S: Ssshh! Listen!

[They both come into the FATHER *who is in the centre and form a protective triangle.]*

*[Image — * FAMILY *security bound by fear.]*

GRETA: What?

MR. S: You hear — he's moving about.

[Move here to stool. They sit silently hearing his scratching up and down the room. Takes his stool upstage, sits.]

He must have woken up.

MRS. S: Poor Gregor! He must be thirsty — he's had nothing to drink all day — I'll give him some milk — he likes milk in the evening. *[Forgetting for a moment his insect state.]* Oh no! *[Starts weeping.]*

GRETA: Mother, that doesn't help, it doesn't help us to be upset — it'll only make him upset too if he hears you.

MRS. S: Yes — you're right — I must be strong — must — be — strong. He'll be hungry too. What do you think he eats?

*[MR. SAMSA *shakes his head in helplessness.]*

Well, give him the milk.

[She mimes bowl of milk — hands it to FATHER *who hands it to* GRETA — GRETA *moves a step upstage and freezes in her tracks.]*

MR. S: Gregor.

*[GRETA *unable to go further.]*

MRS. S: Father! Father, don't let her go in there — take it to him!

MR. S: *[looks sheepish, hating the idea]* Oh, well . . .

GRETA: *[sitting again]* It's all right — I'll do it — just give me a minute more.

MRS. S: How can you sit there and let your daughter go in there?

MR. S: You go in there then — you've been crying over him — he's still your beloved son.

MRS. S: Our son!

MR. S: Our son! You can't call him our son any more —
          not that thing in there! Our son's left us.

MRS. S: Don't say that, he's coming back to us — we can't
          desert him now — he probably needs us more
          than ever. He's so alone — what can he be
          thinking in there, that we find him disgusting —
          we mustn't show him that.

GRETA: We mustn't feel that.

MRS. S: No, never!
          [*Scratching noises.*]

GRETA: Listen, Mother — he's probably starving.

MR. S: [*rising determined*] We'll go . . . with you.

GRETA: [*calls gently through door*] Gregor?
          [*Scratching stops.*]
          Here's some milk for you.
          [*They have all walked upstage to watch* GRETA
          *perform the action of opening the door and shoving the
          saucer in — a hard top light illuminates his room. This
          scene dissolves into his mind's eye. He leaves his cage —
          sliding down and becomes 'normal'. He has returned as*
          GREGOR, *stimulated by the reminder of gentle and past
          reminders of milk.*]

GREGOR: I like milk in the morning — it's my favourite
          drink — Mother leaves it for me every morning at
          four a.m. to catch the five a.m. train — daily.
          [FAMILY *waving goodbye.*]

MR. S: Sell lots, lad.

GREGOR: Goodbye, Father.

GRETA: Good luck, Gregor.

GREGOR: Goodbye, Greta.

MRS. S: Don't forget to drink your milk.

GREGOR: No, Mother.

MRS. S: Nice basin of fresh milk with little white sops of
          bread in it.
          [GREGOR *mimes glass, it turns into a basin, he drinks
          it and spits it out in revulsion — his body changes back
          into insect stance (reminded by bowl).*]

MRS. S: Why isn't he drinking it? [*She is now in the present.*]

MR. S: Come on, son — drink it up.

GRETA: Oh Gregor — you know you like it.

MRS. S: It's your favourite drink.

GRETA: He's probably ashamed to drink it with us list-
           ening to him — let's go away.

           [*They tiptoe downstage and continue moving during
           next speech which marks distance and time.* GREGOR
           *has left the normal state that the milk association first
           drew him to and is back to beetle state.*]

GREGOR: I don't like milk any more — it's revolting to me
           — bring me something more to my taste — you
           don't have to look at me, Greta — I'll hide under
           the bed — but I desperately need some food —
           I'm starving to death!

           [GREGOR *changes, to face upstage. Lights up.*]

           [*The following morning the* FAMILY *are sitting at
           breakfast — they mime actions.*]

MRS. S: [*to* GRETA] Greta . . . ? Have you um . . . ?

GRETA: No — not yet.

           [*Long silence.*]

MRS. S: Did he . . . ?

GRETA: I don't know — I don't know — I haven't looked.

           [*Pause.*]

MRS. S: Would you?

           [GRETA *senses that her mother wishes her to
           look . . . She moves to the cage door, sees him and rushes
           back.*]

MR. S: What is it?

GRETA: He's under the bed.

MR. S: Well, he had to be somewhere. He couldn't fly
           away. Could he?

MRS. S: Did he drink it?

GRETA: He obviously doesn't like it any more.

MRS. S: He's so unhappy — that's why he's not eating.

GRETA: He spilt some milk so obviously he must have
           tried it.

MRS. S: What do you suppose they . . . he eats?

GRETA: I . . . don't know. [*suddenly excited*] I know, we'll
           put out some bits and pieces and then we'll know
           by what he leaves what he likes best.

MR. S: }
MRS. S: } Oh, yes — that's the best thing to do.

           [*The* FAMILY *become united in their new idea — hands*

shoot out collecting, gathering and discovering old scraps.]

GRETA: Some old carrots and greens — potatoes and cauliflowers.

[*Image — the gathering of goodies — each on own stool — making things appear from the air.*]

MRS. S: This cheese is old — I don't suppose anyone would miss it.

MR. S: Here's a stale loaf.

GREGOR: Yes!

MRS. S: A buttered roll.

GREGOR: Yes!

GRETA: Nuts.

GREGOR: Yes!

MRS. S: Raisins.

GREGOR: Yes!

MR. S: Apples.

GREGOR: Yes!

MR. S: That should do.

MRS. S: What about the remains of last night's stew?

GREGOR: Oh yes!

GRETA: It's got some nice white sauce on it. He'll probably like that.

[GRETA *mimes the action of gathering the huge pile that has been found. She carries the food carefully to the door, everybody watches from the front area — she goes in and quickly turns and hurries back. Noise of scurrying and* GREGOR *chewing bone. They are all listening to him.*]

MRS. S: Come, Greta, finish your breakfast — he seems to be enjoying his now — come on, Father. [*They continue eating — the noise of* GREGOR *gets louder.— they stop eating.*] Take no notice of him, Father!

MR. S: It's a bit difficult, isn't it? [*Indicates noise.*]

MRS. S: Well, the only thing to do then is to make more noise than he does — then you won't hear him.

[*She resumes her breakfast noisily — the others follow her example. The sound of eating from both rooms gets louder and louder. Fade as noise dies down.*]

GREGOR: [*stretches in cage . . . bloated*] Oh, I could weep with joy and satisfaction — God, I was starving! I liked the cheese particularly but can't stand the smell

of the fresher food. [*Examines limbs.*] And my
wound's healed — I must be less sensitive — a
cut on my finger once took a whole month.

[*An hour later the* FAMILY *are still sitting. The clock is
ticking and rain is beating on the roof. Odd noises stand
out in the heavy silence. An occasional bark of a dog is
heard to remind one of the existence outside.* FATHER
starts a slow walk up and down between the women.]

MRS. S: He's gone very quiet.

GRETA: Yes.

MRS. S: Do you think there was enough?

GRETA: I think so, he even ate the old bit of cheese.

MRS. S: [*happily*] Oh, good!

GRETA: The rest he left in a pile.

MRS. S: Let's clean his room, Greta. Turn the key slowly
— that's his signal to retreat.

GRETA: He's under the bed again. His body is so swollen,
he can hardly breathe.

MRS. S: Never mind.

GRETA: His eyes are bulging out of his head.

MRS. S: Clean his room — we'll put what he doesn't eat
into a bucket.

[*Image — the cleaning of* GREGOR's *room — the
sweeping — the foul smell as the remains are put into a
bucket — all this done on stools.*]

MR. S: [*Stops pacing and screams.*] Quiet! I don't want to
hear any more — d'you understand me? Do I
make myself clear? No more!

MRS. S: Don't raise your voice in this house!

MR. S: I'll raise my voice if I want to, it's my house — *my
house!* [*Sits downstage centre clutching his stool.*]

MRS. S: Is it? [*Ballet of the stools.*] Gregor installed us here
— as you retired yourself from work, we had to
depend on him for money — we could never have
afforded it without him.

MR. S: A terrible thing if a son supports his parents in
their declining years — I've kept you all long
enough.

GRETA: Please don't, Father — why are you angry — it
doesn't solve anything.

MR. S: I don't care if it solves anything or not — I can't

	sit at the table without hearing him scratching round.
MRS. S:	Greta, in future feed him before we get up.
GRETA:	Yes, Mother.
MRS. S:	We wish to spare your father as much anxiety as possible.
MR. S:	[*slightly abashed — sheepishly*] You know how I look forward to my breakfast — eating the rolls all hot and crisp from the bakery — and the smell of an early morning newspaper and coffee smells — I don't have much in my life to look forward to — but that's one of them.
MRS. S:	Greta won't feed him any more in your presence.
MR. S:	[*rising again*] All right, all right! Don't look at me as if I was some idiot you had to humour.
GRETA:	Don't you think, instead of avoiding the subject, we should discuss it!
MRS. S:	Oh, Greta, how sensible.
GRETA:	You see, if we bring it out into the open, it will not seem so . . . terrible, and we can put our heads together and work out a solution.
MRS. S:	Yes, if we could only do that.
	[*They put their heads together.*]
GREGOR:	Greta took it on herself to take sole charge of me, as she was the only one who dared come into the room and inform the family of my progress.
	[*Loud ticking suggests passing of several days to the next scene.*]
	[GRETA *is seen leaving* GREGOR's *room and entering downstage area. The* FAMILY *are seated.*]
GRETA:	Well, he ate all his dinner today.
	[*They freeze — reaction of joy.*]
GREGOR:	Or . . .
	[GRETA *repeats same business.* FATHER *and* MOTHER *in different positions.*]
	[*Image.*]
GRETA:	Everything's been left standing again.
	[*Dull reaction.*]
	[*Image.*]
GREGOR:	Or . . .
	[*Same business,* FAMILY *in different positions.*]

GRETA: He's not eaten now for two days.
              [MRS. SAMSA *groans. Fade out on freeze of depression.*]
              [*Image — eating — silent mime.*]
GREGOR: *I can hear you!* You think I can't understand you —
              simply because you can't understand me, but I
              can, I can — I can hear every sound you make —
              every moan.
MRS. S: There is one potato left, that's for Father.
              [*Mimes plate which she pushes round the table. She very
              carefully mimes the edge of the plate between forefinger
              and thumb and pushes it away — the heads of the
              FAMILY move in rhythm to the plate so we never 'lose'
              it.*]
GRETA: Yes, go on, Father, you have the last potato.
MR. S: I've had quite sufficient, Mother. Here you are,
              Greta. [*Slides it to her.*]
GRETA: I don't need any more food. I wish you'd eat it,
              Mother.
              [*She returns the potato to MOTHER who refuses it and
              pushes it back to GRETA.*]
MRS. S: I want no more of this silly nonsense.
              [*The potato is pushed round faster and faster until
              eventually GRETA misses it and it falls on the floor.*]
GRETA: Oh, I'm sorry, it was all my fault.
MRS. S: No it wasn't — it's nobody's fault — dear me,
              what a to-do about a potato — it won't go to
              waste — we'll save it for Gregor. [FATHER *glares at
              her — she realizes her blunder.*] Look, Father, why
              don't you let Greta go out and get a beer for you?
GRETA: Yes — let me get a beer, Father — like you used to
              have after supper.
MR. S: No thank you, Greta.
GRETA: Come on — you know you like a beer after your
              supper.
MR. S: If there's not enough money for potatoes, there's
              not enough money for beer.
              [*Loud moan from GREGOR's room.*]
MRS. S: [*whispers*] Did you hear that?
GRETA: Perhaps he can understand what we're saying.
MR. S: Of course not.
GRETA: How do you know? How can you tell? Perhaps he
              listens to us.

MR. S: Then maybe he should listen, won't hurt him to know.

MRS. S: Father!

MR. S: Well, maybe he should know what this indisposition of his has caused us — and then he'd appreciate what we're doing for him and how *we're* suffering on his account.

MRS. S: What about Gregor? I don't suppose you think he's suffering! Shut up in his room — not seeing a soul — not knowing what's going to happen — you owe him a lot, don't forget that.

MR. S: I do!

MRS. S: Yes, all of us. How he toiled day and night to be a commercial traveller — travelling up and down the country to all those awful places to take orders.

    [All sigh.]

GRETA: And the letters he wrote — those miserable letters from those cold hotel rooms.

    [All sigh.]

MRS. S: We simply took it for granted. And how he longed to hear you play the violin again. Yes, always knowing that he would earn enough to support us, and so often he wasn't even home to enjoy it.

    [GREGOR, finding this all too much, gives a loud sigh, but they are too occupied to notice.]

FAMILY: Yes.

MR. S: *[wistfully]* He was becoming a good salesman, that lad — he could've really reached a high position in his firm and earned a royal salary.

MRS. S: And that secret plan to send you to the Conservatorium to study.

    [They all stare ahead, lost in their thoughts. The lights fade. There is a sound of laughter and glasses. As the lights come up, we see GREGOR as he was the Christmas before. The FAMILY are all merry. When GREGOR steps into the past, a strange light illuminates the scene. They pose three times, there are flashes. We see each one as a series of photographs which come to life when GREGOR speaks.]

    [Images — photos: awkwardness, happiness, summer, youth. Kneeling — standing.]

GREGOR: And now I would like to propose a small toast!
            [*Everyone takes glasses.*] First of all: to our dear
            mother for the most wonderful Christmas
            dinners. [*All clap and 'Hear, hear'.*] To our dear
            father — and may he spend his last years com-
            fortably smoking Havana cigars! [*More reaction.*]
            And now a toast to my talented sister and a little
            secret . . .

MRS. S: Oh, Gregor — do tell us, what is it?

GREGOR: Not really sure that I should yet . . .

GRETA: Oh, Gregor, don't be a tease — now you've gone
            so far, you must . . .

GREGOR: Well, I'm determined that one day our little one
            should play the violin in the grand orchestra . . .
            and, despite great expense, I am sending her to
            study at the Conservatorium.

            [*Absolute silence follows this announcement then they
            all speak together.*]

MRS. S: Oh, Gregor, what a wonderful, wonderful thing
            you give us.

GRETA: I can't believe it, my lovely brother, I'm so happy.

MR. S: The Conservatorium! My word! Soon we'll be
            seeing the great Greta Samsa playing at the
            concert hall and saying that's our very own
            daughter.

            [*Images — they watch her playing at the concert — they
            eat chocolates, nervously passing the box — excited by
            GRETA's playing — biting fingernails — and then they
            dance — amidst laughter — cartwheels and somer-
            saults. The music is by Puccini.*]

            [*Everybody get up and hugs GREGOR — violin music
            plays and they all dance. Gradually they dance further
            and further apart until the music slowly winds down.
            They are back in their previous positions.*]

MR. S: Dreams — dreams — he never did send Greta to
            the Conservatorium.

MRS. S: But he meant well.

GREGOR: [*as scene fades*] Why didn't she go? Because you
            took the money . . . you took the money that was
            meant for Greta.

            [*Blackout.*]

[*Image* — FATHER *wrestles with his son — the age-old desire of the father wishing to kill his male off-spring.* GREGOR *is thrown into his cage.*]

[*Lights hard on in this scene as if a reflection of the previous thought.*]

MR. S: Investments . . . ! That certain investments have survived the wreck of our misfortune.

GRETA:
MRS. S: } Yes . . . ?

MR. S: The money that Gregor brought home was not used after all — I had been shrewd enough at the time to invest some of it . . .

GRETA:
MRS. S: } Yes, yes . . . ?

MR. S: [*holding up a letter*] And now the brokers inform me that the investments have grown!

MRS. S: Oh, Father — how fortunate — we're beginning to need so many things.

[*Image* — MOTHER *and* DAUGHTER *buying, trying on hats, giggling — hope — running through huge shopping emporium.*]

MR. S: Whilst, however, it is sufficient for the rent, etc., as well as putting some by for a rainy day . . .

GRETA:
MRS. S: } Yes, that's most important.

MR. S: It'll still be necessary to earn enough for our expenses.

MRS. S: Of course.

GRETA: Let me work! I'm longing to go out to work.

MR. S: Yes, you could always take in washing as your mother did in the bad old days.

MRS. S: But it's only till Gregor gets better.

[*Image* — *the store disappears* — *hat is removed.*]

MR. S: We don't know that.

[*Gasps as he realizes what he has just said.* GREGOR *twists in cage.* FAMILY *slowly sink, their faces pulled into masks of terror. Long silence.*]

MRS. S: Taking in washing won't bring in much.

MR. S: I'll help until I find a little job — the old brain hasn't quite gone rusty — might do some book-keeping or stock-checking at a warehouse. I should have started fresh again instead of depending on him.

MRS. S: Who was to know?

MR. S: I should have! There was always something about Gregor that was strange.

MRS. S: Gregor! Strange!

MR. S: Gregor, yes, Gregor — although he worked hard, he never seemed to be a part of it — don't think he wanted to — stood outside it somehow — as if he was saying: "This is nothing to do with me" . . . he didn't really like work, he downright resented it.

MRS. S: How can you say that when he worked so hard?

MR. S: Oh, I know he worked hard — but did you ever see his face sometimes after he'd come home, it was hard with resentment — saying, it's for you I'm doing this.

MRS. S: Stop feeling guilty, Father, because we lived off him — he kept this house from crumbling!

MR. S: I don't want to hear you talking like that.

MRS. S: If he toiled and slaved at something he resented, perhaps that's why he's left us now!

[*Image — the two women start trembling — fists raised,* FATHER *primed to destroy.*]

[*Their eyes lock in mutual hatred. Sound of whispering from room. They go to separate areas and take on attitude of sleep.*]

GRETA: Goodnight, Father . . . Mother.

GREGOR: I've not left you — I'm coming back soon — I didn't resent anything, even if I didn't keep much money for myself, I didn't resent it. Oh God, you make me so ashamed, I could hide away for ever. If only I could speak to you, if I could thank you Greta for looking after me, perhaps you'd all get used to me — I can't stand just silence — I must speak — I must — I must gather all my strength together and speak to her.

MRS. S: [*from sleep area*] It's time to feed him, Greta.

[GRETA *goes to his room — she is about to enter when* GREGOR *stands up and attempts to speak but only succeeds in making a strangling sound.*]

GRETA: Oh, no, no. [*Rushes away.*]

GREGOR: I won't try to speak again — I know I'm repulsive and I'll go on being repulsive — how brave you are Greta to come here at all — don't come any more. I don't like you, Greta, opening my window twice a day as if there were some intolerable stench in here — why did you run away like that — you should be used to me by now . . . (*Anyone would think I was lying in wait to bite you.*)

GRETA: He must be terribly lonely — he tried to speak to me . . . but he couldn't — he could only make a squeaking noise and I ran out, as if he were something filthy and disgusting, my own Gregor.

MRS. S: You're very brave, Greta.

GRETA: Usually he hides from me before I clear his room as if he knows how loathsome he is.

MRS. S: She's very good to him the way she ministers to him.

GRETA: But today he just stood there in front of me — I felt sick.

MR. S: Perhaps he was trying to thank her — he was always very polite.

GRETA: He just stares out of the window — stares out at his old world.

GREGOR: It's growing dimmer — it looks like a desert waste of grey sky and grey land — everything's grey . . . everything.
　　　[*Fade.*]

New scene almost sub-titled 'Optimism'. They are all gay in spirits since they expect a change in fortune. They practically dance the opening — MR. SAMSA has found a job.

MR. S: All right . . . ! Up we get.
　　　[*The* FAMILY *are all working on polishing the brasswork on* MR. SAMSA's *uniform as a bank messenger.*]

GRETA: [*looking into button*] I can see my face clearly.

MRS. S: They certainly give you a smart uniform.
　　　[MR. SAMSA *is getting ready, combing his hair and preening himself.*]

MR. S: [*jovially*] I suppose the lowly office of bank messenger entitles you to look like a general.

GRETA: There we are — all ready.

[*They dress him with elaborate care. Objects are drawn in space and thrown to him.*]

MRS. S: }
GRETA: } Hat! Coat! Gloves!

MRS. S: Oh, Father! How handsome you look.

MR. S: Are you sure you'll be all right whilst I'm out?

GRETA: }
MRS. S: } Of course we will.

MR. S: I don't like leaving you two alone in the house.

MRS. S: Oh, Father, we're perfectly safe.

GRETA: Gregor's no trouble, he's not going to bite us.

[*Image — music changes. They become involved in their own thoughts and drift apart — the room becomes heavy and dark and oppressive, the cage at the back is lit as though by silent coloured lighting — their motions increase in weight and intensity — GREGOR slowly climbs up the walls of his cage — the FAMILY seem contaminated by GREGOR, particularly GRETA.*]

MR. S: What's he been doing?

GRETA: He seems to be sleeping a lot — at least he's very quiet and he's been eating all his food.

MR. S: Humph!

GRETA: Sometimes he likes to look out of the window — I know he does that because I hear him creep under the bed when he hears me opening the door, just so I shouldn't see him.

MRS. S: Poor, poor Gregor — he must be so lonely and bored.

GRETA: No, I don't think he is. Lately he's formed the habit of crawling over the walls and ceiling.

MR. S: How do you know? You're surely not in there when he does it.

GRETA: [*During her speech GREGOR has started very slowly to climb his cage.*] Oh, no, he leaves traces — like footprints, from the sticky stuff on his feet — I think he likes hanging from the ceiling best — it makes him feel free and light, he doesn't have much room on the floor.

MRS. S: I must go in and see him — perhaps he needs me.

MR. S: In his state all he wants is feeding — he probably wouldn't thank you to have you see him like that.

[*Image — the lights and obsessional quality of everyone changes and normalizes.*]

MRS. S: But he is still my son — don't you understand? No matter what happens he is my unfortunate child and I must see him. [*She suddenly breaks away.*]

MR. S: If you behave like this, I'll throw off my coat and stay here!

MRS. S: [*resigned*] No . . . No . . . I shan't go in — I don't think I could bear it. Go to work, Father — you look very smart — don't you worry about me.

MR. S: Understand, dear, that it's for your own good.

MRS. S: Yes, yes, yes.

MR. S: [*to* GRETA] Hold on to the key.

GRETA: Yes, Father.

[*He goes.*]

[*Image — the listless automatic waving as* FATHER *leaves and a strong light revealing the swaying huge body of the* GREGOR *beetle — the anticipation of horror.*]

[*By this time* GREGOR *has climbed on to the ceiling of his cage and just hangs there.* MOTHER *and* GRETA *are waving goodbye to* FATHER. GREGOR *speaks, rocking in time to the waves. (This speech is a grim fore-shadowing of events and the separation of animal from human. The acceptance of his state which now almost gives him pleasure. Hang your legs over the cross bar and cup your toes into the side bars to give your body a braced, arched look.)*]

GREGOR: I liked hanging from the ceiling. It was better than the floor — one breathed more freely — and I can swing and rock backwards and forwards, forwards and backwards — I feel so light, and I can see the hospital across the street — all I can see from the floor is a drab, grey sky — I so much want to see my mother — it's so long since I've seen her — perhaps I'm too hideous ever to see her again.

MRS. S: You think he's well, you say?

GRETA: He seems to be. I don't hear him moan like he did.

MRS. S: But you said he didn't have enough room.

GRETA: No, I don't think he does. I want to shift some
          furniture so that he can move around more
          easily.

MRS. S: It's so heavy you'll never manage it alone.

GRETA: Father'll help me.

MRS. S: Your father'll never go in there.

GRETA: Then I'll shift it myself.

MRS. S: Listen, Greta — I'll help you. Please understand
          how necessary it is for a mother to see her son —
          no matter what, and perhaps how necessary it is
          for him to see her — so we'll just shift some of the
          furniture that hinders him before Father comes
          back.

GRETA: Are you sure?

MRS. S: Yes, yes — let us go in and be quite matter-of-fact
          about it.

              [*Hearing this* GREGOR *drops down.*]

              [*Image — the terror and fear as they move like the base
              of a triangle shortening to its point.*]

GRETA: Wait . . . what do you think we should take first?

MRS. S: Oh yes, we must decide now — we mustn't upset
          him — let's take the chest.

GRETA: That's heavy.

MRS. S: All right, his writing desk.

GREGOR: *Leave it!*

MRS. S: Oh, Greta — that desk was his ever since primary
          school — he used to build models on it, and all
          those hours of homework he's toiled on that
          desk.

GRETA: When he's better we'll put it back.

MRS. S: What about his bed — he doesn't really need that
          now.

GREGOR: *Yes, I need that to hide under — Leave it!*

GRETA: All right, let's go in.

MRS. S: [*whispers*] Doesn't it look by taking all his furni-
          ture that we're giving up all hope of his recovery?

GRETA: No, of course not — he'll think we're trying to
          help.

MRS. S: Oh, I don't know — wouldn't it be better to leave
          the room alone — then when he recovers, he'll
          find it exactly as it was, and he'll forget more
          easily what happened in between.

GRETA: I don't agree with you, Mother — I always hear
          him bumping into things . . . all right now, let's
          begin.
                    [*Image — in slow motion as he speaks they are
                    emptying his room in unison while* GREGOR's *fear
                    increases.*]
GREGOR: You're turning my room into a naked den for
          some wild beast to roam in — leave it. If you
          empty my room I'll forget who I am, I'll lose all
          recollection of my humanity — *I'll become what I
          am* — no, no, it mustn't happen . . . they'll take
          my picture frame with the lady in the fur muff —
          they mustn't take that!
                    [GREGOR *lets himself come into full view and attacks
                    them, spitting with rage.*]
MRS. S: Oh God . . . no!
GRETA: Mother . . . Mother! [*Holds her up.*] Gregor! [*Shakes
          fist at him.*]
MR. S: [*rushing in*] What's happening?
GRETA: Gregor's broken loose.
MR. S: I expected this to happen.
GRETA: He just rushed at us.
                    [*Image —* GREGOR *escapes — the world caves in —
                    the women are moving as if in a ship hurled by a storm
                    —* MR. SAMSA *comes in —* GREGOR *hides under the
                    table — we know he's under a table but the* FAMILY
                    *can't see him — they peek under the tablecloth. They lift
                    an imaginary table — he hides again, under a stool. The
                    furniture the* FAMILY *shift illustrates* GREGOR's *size.
                    The* FAMILY *spin around as he appears as if dazzled by
                    his ugliness — eventually the* FATHER *mimes an apple
                    from a bowl.*]
GRETA: I think he's under the sofa. Don't hurt him.
MR. S: Apple for you, Gregor.
                    [*He hurls it —* GREGOR *frantically claws the floor,
                    not knowing whether to go back or to go forward.*]
GRETA: Escape, Gregor — escape!
MR. S: Scaring people to death!
GRETA: Do go forward, Gregor — he'll hit you!
MR. S: [*throwing*] And another!
MRS. S: Climb, Gregor — climb the walls — you can
          climb!

MR. S: I'll hit him! It's sunk in!

> [GREGOR *screams, falls on his back, legs waving in the air, unable to find his balance.*]

Back! Back! Back! Back!

> [MR. SAMSA *throws a missile with each scream of 'back' —* GREGOR *heaves himself back into his cage.*]

> [MOTHER *and* DAUGHTER *now seize hold of* FATHER *— a terrible light illuminates the scene as if the* FAMILY *are lit by strokes of lightning — huge beetle shadows of the group downstage — slide and shudder over the cyclorama. Their faces are torn open in silent screams. A strange music reflects the torment, twisting and jangling.*]

MRS. S: [*Recovered now but horrified she throws herself round* MR. SAMSA'*s neck.*] No, Father! No! No! No! Stop it for God's sake, you're killing my son.

> [GRETA *and* MRS. SAMSA *prevent him from beating* GREGOR *any more.* MR. SAMSA *takes women and starts spinning them like tops.*]

MR. S: It's all right.

> [GREGOR *slowly crawls back to his room, slow fade as we hear him whimpering.*]

He's gone back.

GREGOR: [*as light slowly illuminates the cage*] Could that have been you, Father — you used to lie so wearily sunk in your bed as I set off to work, you used to welcome me when I returned still in your dressing gown, you who could never rise to your feet but could only lift a feeble arm —

> [*Image —* GREGOR *walks with them in memory of the slow Sunday procession to church — slow motion.*]

Who, on Sundays walked between me and my mother, shuffling along with your stick at an even slower rate than us. Where did you get such strength . . . ? You threw that apple so hard, it sank into my back!

New scene. Lights up on the FAMILY. FATHER *is nodding off, coming to an abrupt awakening each time.* MOTHER *is sewing,* GRETA *is studying French lessons. All their movements should be orchestrated and mechanical.*

GRETA: Je suis, tu es, il est — nous sommes, vous êtes, ils sont; je vais, tu vas, il va . . .

MR. S: [*awakening*] Greta, you've been saying those verbs for the last three hours — isn't it time you gave it a rest?

MRS. S: [*whispering*] Look at him — the great General — [GRETA *mouths words again.*] Just reads the paper and sleeps — doesn't care that you want to improve yourself — Oh, I can't stand him looking like that — all unshaven and scruffy.

    [*Clock strikes ten.* MR. SAMSA *jerks awake.*]

    Come, Father — you'll not sleep properly there — let's get you to bed. [*Attempts to get him up.*]

MR. S: Leave me alone!

MRS. S: Look at yourself sleeping in your nice smart uniform — you never take it off any more. What must they think of you at the bank?

MR. S: If I want to wear it all the time, it's my business. [*Sinks into chair.*]

MRS. S: Come on, Greta — help me!

    [*They take an arm each and put him to bed.*]

MR. S: [*as he is led out*] This is the life — this is the peace and quiet of my o-o-o-o-l-l-l-d-d-d age.

    [*He sleeps standing, arms wrapped over each other. They tiptoe away.*]

MRS. S: [*whispering*] What's he doing?

GRETA: I think he's sleeping — the apple's still sunk in his back.

MRS. S: Oh dear — I hoped he'd be able to get rid of it — you remember how quickly his other wound healed.

GRETA: He can't reach round to his back.

MRS. S: Oh Greta, can't you try and do something?

GRETA: The apple . . . ? [*as she thinks of* GREGOR's *festering back*] — I can't . . . I just can't do that, Mother!

MRS. S: I would, but I'm afraid of fainting.

GRETA: I'll do it — he's not used to having anyone else there but me.

MRS. S: Then do it, please Greta — otherwise he'll think we don't care any more.

GRETA: [*hard — impatiently*] Yes, I'll do it tomorrow.

    [GRETA *goes to sleep, stage right, whilst* MRS. SAMSA *walks downstage to centre stool and just sits.*]

Gregor's Dream

A strange light filters gradually on to the stage — hardening and elongating features — GREGOR's heart is heard beating, the lights adjust to the heartbeats — the movement of the FAMILY seems caught in the motion of the beat — the bodies occasionally pulled by its sound — they appear as if under water.

GREGOR: [*Screams, drained of any energy.*] The apple's still inside me — I can't move any more — I can't climb — it takes me ages to crawl under the bed.

MRS. S: His room's filthy, Greta — he's lying there in heaps of filth and dust.

GRETA: I'm tired — I'm tired of working — trudging out my life in a shop all day.

MRS. S: We mustn't leave him — he'll think we don't care any more.

GREGOR: Take it out of me — I can feel it beginning to rot — it's becoming inflamed — covered with dust.

MRS. S: Oh, Greta, do something.

GRETA: I can't, Mother, I can't do that.

MRS. S: Father, do something.
   [*Image — FATHER laughs — the pulse of the heart and light snatches the reason from his voice — the words break. End. Shudder — again automation from GREGOR.*]

MR. S: He's a dung beetle — he's just a dung beetle.
   [*Cry is heard — they twist around in their sleep.*]

MRS. S: We mustn't hurt him any more — he's still our son.

MR. S: No, not that thing in there, our son's left us.

GREGOR: I'm hungry — oh, I'm so hungry.

MRS. S: Feed him, Greta — you're not feeding him any more.

GRETA: I do feed him — I've always fed him.
   [*Image — a giant beetle composed of the FAMILY, the arms moving in stiff staccato rhythm, and bodies twist and join together in agonized conflict.*]

GREGOR: Yes — any old scraps of food without considering what I like — just throw something in — slam the door and leave me in the darkness again.

GRETA: He would probably have perished without me.

MRS. S: I wish we could move to a smaller house — we could save so much money.

MR. S: How could we move that creature in there without anybody noticing — no, there's nothing we can do. But work — we must work.

[*They all continue with the same word, fading out on it.*]

GREGOR: [*As he speaks, the* FAMILY *hold their positions like a fresco.*] Of course you could move me. You could shift me in a box with air holes — no — you're blaming me for your own helplessness.

Phase Three

MR. S: Work, Gregor. Time to get up.

[*Image — the beetle dissolves, the limbs disconnect. Dreamlike,* GREGOR *walks to work,* MR. SAMSA *hangs upside down in the cage, the pace increases, maddens.*]

GRETA: Time, Gregor — four a.m. — you must catch the five a.m. train.

MR. S: [*Pulls* GREGOR *out of cage.*] Pack your samples — come on Gregor, don't be lazy.

[GREGOR *now starts walking on the spot.*]

MRS. S: He works so hard — he's good to us.

GRETA: You must hurry, Gregor, hurry — I need violin lessons.

MRS. S: Only five years to go, Gregor.

GREGOR: Yes!

MR. S: What will the Chief Clerk say if you're late?

GREGOR: Yes!

MRS. S: Oh, Gregor, hurry! Hurry! Hurry!

[*They repeat their phrases faster and faster.* FATHER *is in the cage now — whipping him on —* MOTHER *and* GRETA *have stood on their stools as if on a grandstand.* GREGOR *moves faster — the heartbeat accelerates — suddenly* GREGOR'*s movements become jerky, mechanical. He breaks into a run — but a strange hideous run like a beetle scurrying along with a ball of dung — he now moves as a sprinter, so fast it seems his heart will*] *burst. He stops, exhausted.* FATHER *draws his arm back to the whine of the women and throws his apple.* GREGOR *screams, transfixed — a single spot emphasizes his agony — slowly his body transforms itself, trembling jerkily into* SAMSA/INSECT — *his arms crossed — fingers bent like hooks — he collapses over a stool — he now appears less human than insect — the* FAMILY *come downstage and look at him as if witnessing a street accident — they whisper in uninvolved concern.* GRETA *and* FATHER *walk to their sleeping positions.* MOTHER *above, takes him slowly back to his cage.*]

MRS. S: Don't worry, Gregor — you're not being forgotten by your old mother — she'll look after you if nobody else does — have it all clean for you to roam around in — don't worry, we won't have a charlady in here — nobody'll have to see you. You'll soon be well — I can feel it — as soon as the weather starts to break and the cold winds go — we'll have a bit of spring in the air and one morning you will wake up and see that it's been a nasty dream.

          [*Image —* MRS. SAMSA *takes him back to his room — gently reassuring this is* GREGOR — *tired, old.*]

          [*End of dream sequence. Fade to darkness. Silence. The lights hard up, morning.*]

          [*Three loud knocks.*]

MR. S: That will be the lodgers for the room!
          [*These* THREE LODGERS *can be played by one.*]

MRS. S: Lodgers!
MR. S: Cash!
MRS. S: Lodgers!
GRETA: Shoes!
MRS. S: Lodgers!
MR. S: Beer!
MRS. S: Lodgers!
GRETA: Books!
MRS. S: Lodgers!
MR. S: Cigars!
MRS. S: Lodgers!
GRETA: Clothes!
MRS. S: [*ecstatic*] Lodgers . . . Sir, do come in.

[*Three men in white harlequins' masks behind each other in exact step as if one person. They copy each other's every move — over-react to everything — concerned for their welfare totally and are greedy. The pig faces of the harlequin masks exactly externalize their inner state. They move fast, acrobatically and energetically.*]

1ST L: It's warm.

2ND L: Pleasant.

3RD L: A little cramped, but it'll do.
[*They all take the family stools.*]

MRS. S: We'll try and make it comfortable.

MR. S: It's a very friendly household — say the word and we'll do our best.

GRETA: [*giggling*] What funny faces!

MRS. S: Ssshhh!

1ST L: We'd like to be called at eight o'clock.

2ND L: Prompt!

3RD L: Breakfast hot and ready at eight fifteen!

2ND L: Prompt!

1ST L: Coffee, rolls and cheese.

2ND L: Marmalade, if you please.

3RD L: And toast.

MRS. S: I think we'll manage that all right.

1ST L: We're sticklers for order.

2ND L: Especially in the kitchen.

3RD L: Can't bear slovenliness.

MRS. S: You tell us what you need.

1ST L: When we've examined our quarters.

2ND L: We'll tell you all of our objections.

MR. S: [*uncomfortably*] Hmmph! [*clearing his throat*] There's er . . . one thing you should know before you make a decision.

1ST L: Yes?

MR. S: We . . . er . . . keep a pet in the back room.

ALL L'S: Oh yes?

MR. S: I wondered if that would bother you?

ALL L'S: Oh no, we're fond of pets.

MRS. S: I'll show you to your quarters and then you can have some supper. [*She takes them out . . . as she returns*] They seem quite . . .

MR. S: I hope they don't . . . [*Indicates* GREGOR*'s room.*]

MRS. S: I shouldn't think they'd . . .

MR. S: Mind?

MRS. S: No!

MR. S: Let's hope he doesn't . . .

MRS. S: Of course he won't.

[The LODGERS return.]

1ST L: It suits us moderately well.

2ND L: Except for these articles which we would like to dispose of.

ALL L'S: Please.

[They all raise arms indicating objects.]

MR. S: Greta! Take the lodgers' belongings with you and put them away somewhere.

[They pass the objects to her and she goes away to GREGOR's room and throws them in — GREGOR shrinks back. Meanwhile, the LODGERS are taking their seats.]

GREGOR: Go on, use my room as a junk room. Make the lodgers the chief consideration. Throw food into me, when you remember. You don't speak of me any more — I still would, after a rare night's sleep, wake up, and imagine I was Gregor — I still hope.

[Fade.]

[The LODGERS are still seated downstage eating. The FAMILY wait on them as servants.]

MR. S: Is it more tasty now?

1ST L: I think so. *[passing plate]*

2ND L: Much better.

3RD L: You're learning . . .

[SECOND LODGER carves joint with elaborate care. Mime carving of meat with hot meat slipping about on the plates — hot potatoes eaten with gulps of breath to cool them down, vegetables spilling on table, etc.]

The potatoes are hot.

1ST L: Hmmmm! It's delicious.

2ND L: Nice and juicy.

[MRS. SAMSA looks on, pleased. They continue eating with refinement — from GREGOR's room can be heard noises of crunching of teeth as GREGOR chews food. Every time this happens the LODGERS stop eating — listen for a moment till crunching stops, then shrug

shoulders and carry on — after the third interruption . . .]

MRS. S: Don't let that disturb you, it's his feeding time.

1ST L: I see, well in future do you think you could stagger our meals?

2ND L: It would be preferable . . .

3RD L: To that hideous noise.

MRS. S: Certainly, certainly — I'm sorry it disturbed you, but I hope you enjoyed the meal?

[*They all look up at her and then get into a whispering huddle — the* FAMILY *look on anxiously — after a few seconds during which each one has looked up and turned back, as if to make up his mind about some fresh point . . .*]

ALL L'S: [*smiling*] Excellent!

[*The* FAMILY *sigh in relief —* GRETA *goes upstage to play her violin — as soon as* GRETA *crooks her arm into the position of playing the violin we hear 'The Blue Danube' being played. The* THREE LODGERS *hear it and react with glee and excitement — they start dancing with their stools and waltzing wildly round the room.*]

MR. S: Is the violin playing disturbing you, gentlemen?

2ND L: On the contrary, we find it enchanting!

[*The* THREE LODGERS *freeze into absurd positions as if caught by a high speed camera — the* FAMILY *on the other side listening attentively.*]

GREGOR: I'm not an animal — I can *hear* the music. No-one in that room can appreciate music like me. Stop playing, spit at these intruders, Greta — play only for me. I'll protect you from these swine — my ugliness could protect you by frightening them away, then I will send you — I announce to you all — I will send you to the Conservatorium! Yes, I know I'm covered in grime and muck — and you all detest me — but I *was* sending Greta to the Conservatorium, but for my mishap, last Christmas — Oh! Was it so long?

[GREGOR *slides into the room. The tableau bursts into life. He is seen by the* FIRST LODGER.]

1ST L: Mr. Samsa!

[*Points at* GREGOR — *music stops — silence —* LODGERS *look at one another, smiling.*]

2ND L: Good God!

3RD L: What a sight!

     [*Image* — GREGOR *is spreadeagled on the floor —
tired, aching, being partially concealed by the skirts of
the women.*]

MR. S: Gentlemen, gentlemen — please do not be
disturbed by what you see, I can only offer my
humblest apologies and assure you it will never
happen again. [*glancing at wife*] Never!

     [LODGERS *seem rather amused by* GREGOR.]

     Now, if you would kindly go to your room . . .

     [LODGERS *consider that they should be angry.*]

1ST L: I see — just like that!

2ND L: No explanation!

3RD L: Nothing!

MR. S: Somebody must have left his door open, but we'll
keep it firmly locked in future.

     [FATHER *has stepped between them and* GREGOR,
*attempting to hide him and at the same time to shepherd
them out.*]

1ST L: And are we expected to live with that creature at
the end of the corridor?

2ND L: He might escape in the night and creep into our
room and attack us in the dark!

MR. S: Please, gentlemen, please! I assure you that no
such thing is possible — he is very mild and quite
weak as he hasn't been too well lately.

1ST L: [*satirically*] Oh! Nothing serious, I hope!

MR. S: Oh no — some digestion trouble, no doubt.

2ND L: No doubt!

1ST L: [*interrupts*] But that doesn't explain your conduct
in not informing me before we took the room that
you kept a zoo.

MR. S: I did say a pet . . .

1ST L: Look at it — it's probably suffering from diseases!

2ND L: He said himself it's not well.

3RD L: He's probably mephitic!

1ST L: Coprolitic!

2ND L: He's a dung beetle!

MR. S: [*struggling*] He's really very tame.

1ST L: Pestilence and dysentery!

2ND L: We'll get cankered and decrepit!

3RD L: Deteriorate!

2ND L:.   And die!

1ST L: It's a dangerous place to live in!

MR. S: [*pushing them away from* GREGOR] Gentlemen, I assure you, you'll be comfortable and need have no fear — you'll never see him again, and now will you please leave the room so that I can clear him away.

    [LODGERS *get into huddle.*]

1ST L: I beg to announce that because of the disgusting conditions prevailing in this household and family [*spits*] I give you my notice on the spot. Naturally I shall not pay you a penny for leaving without notice or for the food I've eaten — on the contrary, I shall consider bringing an action for damages against you!

2ND L: }
3RD L: }   And we, too, give our notice on the spot!

    [*They march off.* MR. SAMSA *staggers to a chair groping through space as if he were being attacked by a vacuum, sits in the chair numbed.* GRETA, *who has been standing with her head down weeping, looks at* GREGOR — GREGOR *just remains where he is.* GRETA *slowly raises her head, suddenly aged and determined. They walk downstage away from* GREGOR, *who remains in the room, gasping for air as he is now very weak.*]

GRETA: [*quietly*] We must get rid of it — I won't utter my brother's name in the presence of this creature — so all I say is get rid of it. We've tried to look after it and to put up with it as far as is humanly possible — I don't think anyone would reproach us in the slightest —

MR. S: My child, I understand all this but what can we do? [GRETA *shrugs in helplessness.*] If only he could understand us. [GRETA *shakes her head to indicate how unthinkable the idea is now.*] If he could understand us — then perhaps we could come to some agreement with him — but as it is there is not much we can do.

GRETA: Yes, yes, you can, Father — you must get rid of the idea that he is Gregor — the fact that we've believed it all this time is the root of our trouble — of course it's not Gregor — if it were he'd have gone away — he'd have known that human beings can't live with such a creature — so, we wouldn't have a brother, but we'd honour his memory. This creature persecutes us — drives our lodgers away and obviously wants the whole apartment to himself and wouldn't care if we slept in the gutter — Oh! Just look at him now!

> [GREGOR *is turning round to go back to his room. This involves much effort and panting.* GRETA *runs behind her* FATHER.]

MR. S: [*gently*] Ssshhh! He's going to his room.

> [*They all watch him silently, as painfully and laboriously he makes his way back. He slowly crawls up on to his cage —* the FAMILY, *unable to endure any more, turn away as if to spare* GREGOR *further agony.*]

GREGOR: I felt their eyes on me to the last, full of fears and misery. I sensed the growing agony of their burden and knew I had to disappear. My aching body seems glad to release the life that keeps it bound in agony — the will to keep it is weakening — and Gregor is flying out — I thought of my family only with tenderness and love.

> [*Cold single light illuminates* GREGOR, *three o'clock strikes and* GREGOR *senses death claiming him.*]

MRS. S: He looked at me — just as we closed the door — he turned his head — his eyes — Gregor's eyes, full of agony, looked at me in such a way as only a child looks at his mother as if to say — no more — no more pain — I sensed his spirit creeping out of him, reluctant to inhabit such a painful dwelling, releasing him, go Gregor, go — bear no hatred for me — forgive — be free, be free my little boy . . . free . . . free.

GREGOR: [*intones with her*] Free . . . free.

MRS. S: [*as the last faint whisper is expelled from* GREGOR] Dead . . .

MR. S: [*walking downstage in a pool of light with* GRETA — *they are entirely isolated from* GREGOR's *death, whose cage light has gone out*] Well now, thanks be to God.

GRETA: Did you see how thin he'd become — it's such a long time since he ate anything.

MR. S: You know what we're going to do today — we're going to take the day off — we'll write letters to our respective employers and take a long stroll in the morning sunshine because that's what we need.

MRS. S: Father, that would be so good.

MR. S: They have returned to me.

[*Taking their hands, they hold his as if they had no other means of life — attempting somehow to kindle a new life force through the current of their bodies.*]

MRS. S: What a lovely peace rests in my heart.

MR. S: We'll sit in a tram and go into the open country with the warm sunshine flooding the windows.

MRS. S: Our jobs really aren't so bad and might lead to better things.

GRETA: I want to leave this house for ever.

MR. S: We'll get a small house — it'll be cheaper and easier to run — probably the one Gregor selected — we could afford it now. How pretty my daughter's become.

MRS. S: My daughter has bloomed into a pretty girl.

GRETA: My body has grown.

MRS. S: It will soon be time.

MR. S: We must find a good husband for her.

[MR. *and* MRS. SAMSA, *sensing each other's thoughts, turn to look at* GRETA — *she releases their hands and stretches — their smiles confirm their thoughts are in harmony — slow fade.*]

The crocuses will just be coming out.

[*Final spot lingers on* GREGOR.]

THE END

Steven Berkoff on *In the Penal Colony*

IN THE PENAL COLONY is a strange tale of torture and suffering. The Officer wishes to preserve his way of life and the punishments that were a 'feature' of the Colony and which attracted in the past such avid response. A machine so fiendish and diabolical that its blueprints could have been designed in Hell.

The story is part fantasy and part allegory and how perceptive of Kafka to have anticipated the scientific cruelties that were to be part of the age to come. The machine is lovingly described and with such a reverence for its technical ingenuity that any suffering the victim experiences is merely an adjunct to it.

I chose to adapt the story and stick faithfully to the text since it contains the drama and unfolds very carefully, building the tension only gradually. There was little to do except put Kafka's words in the mouths of the characters since there is probably more dialogue here than is usual in his stories. The only real invention is the machine or 'harrow'. Such a macabre instrument is best described with words. However, I did commission a machine that was built and designed by Alistair Merry. It was constructed with a thoroughness and detail that only an architect could devise. He followed very closely the description in the story and the machine was suitably frightening.

On that fateful morning in April 1968 we dragged the machine into the Arts Lab, then Jim Haynes' hothouse of emerging radical artists. I will never forget the look on Jim's face as he watched the monster being hauled into the theatre. It was my first production. The play only ran 45 minutes and was a perfect late-night show. Later Haynes decided to make it into a double bill with Kafka's *Report to an Academy*, expertly played by Tutte Lemkow.

It was an eventful time and the Arts Lab provided a sanctuary for odd, unique or wayward artists in a way that no theatre quite manages to do today. — Thanks, Jim Haynes.

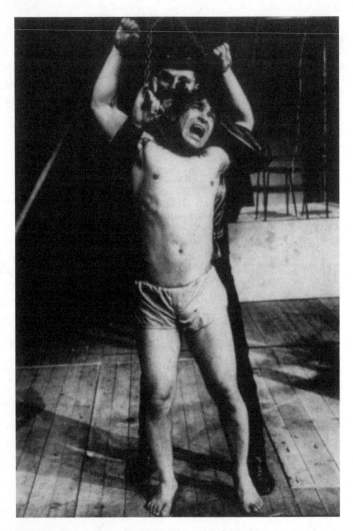
The condemned man is chained to the Guard.
(*Photograph: Cordelia Weedon*)

IN THE PENAL COLONY

In the Penal Colony was first performed at the Arts Laboratory, Drury Lane in London in April, 1968 with the following cast:

THE OFFICER .... Steven Berkoff
THE EXPLORER .... Christopher Heywood
THE PRISONER .... Dino Shafeek
THE GUARD .... Asher Tsarfati

Directed by Steven Berkoff

Design and Construction by Alistair Merry

CHARACTERS

THE OFFICER	Intense, Germanic, younger than he looks — he is perhaps thirty-five.
THE EXPLORER	Cultivated and intelligent — somewhat on edge. He does not like the situation in which he finds himself but is seeking to keep his feelings under control. He, presumably, is in his fifties.
THE PRISONER	Hangdog and unkempt. Of uncertain age.
THE GUARD	A tough, indifferent soldier.

THE TIME	Any time
THE PLACE	A penal colony

Stark noon heat — a bare valley — hot white light. In the centre stage is an apparatus which resembles a bed except that it has straps. A low wooden canopy and various bits of machinery are attached to it — it is used as an instrument of torture. A German OFFICER is explaining the machine to an English EXPLORER. The condemned man (PRISONER) is chained to the GUARD.

The scene takes place on the outskirts of a German military camp somewhere in the tropics.

The OFFICER is in full dress uniform, epaulettes, boots, etc. He sweats under the glare. He proudly surveys the machine, making last-minute adjustments.

OFFICER: It's a remarkable piece of apparatus.

EXPLORER: Hmmm . . .

[*He follows the OFFICER round the machine. The PRISONER's eyes follow their movements as far as his chains will permit. As he does not understand English he tries to interpret the situation through their gestures. He wears an expression of a submissive dog. His chains are attached to his neck, wrist and ankles.*]

OFFICER: [*crawling from underneath the machine — to absorb the sweat he has two ladies' handkerchiefs tucked inside his collar*] I think we're almost ready now.

EXPLORER: [*surveying the OFFICER's sweaty face*] Rather heavy for the tropics — your uniform, I mean.

OFFICER: [*having expected comments of praise for the apparatus he i·dismissive — washes his hands in bucket*] Yes . . . yes, of course — but it means home to us — we don't want to forget about home, do we? [*dries hands*] Now look at this machine — up to now everything has been set by hand, but now it works automatically — it's ready, poised for action — take a seat. [*hands wicker chair to EXPLORER — there are dozens littered round the edge of the stage*] Things sometimes go wrong, of course — we're not infallible but let's hope that nothing goes wrong today — I don't know if the Commandant has explained the apparatus to you . . .

[*The EXPLORER makes a vague gesture.*]

It consists, as you see, of three parts — familiarity

has given them popular nicknames — [*laughs*] — the lower one is called the 'bed', the upper the 'designer', and the middle section the 'harrow'.

EXPLORER: [*vaguely wiping his brow*] A harrow?

OFFICER: You're hot — the sun's too strong for you delicate northerners.

EXPLORER: [*shading his eyes*] It's really the glare — it makes it difficult to collect one's thoughts . . . about the harrow —

OFFICER: Yes, the harrow! A good name for it, no? The needles are set in like a harrow except that this is far more artistic — I'll describe the apparatus before I set it in motion — you'll follow the proceedings better. The condemned man is laid face down on the bed, which is completely covered by cotton wool . . .

    [*The* EXPLORER *reacts.*]

I'll tell you why later — here are the straps for the hands and feet and neck to hold him fast — the felt gag at the head of the bed prevents him from screaming and biting his tongue — he's forced to take the gag into his mouth or his neck would be broken by the strap.

EXPLORER: [*bending forward, becoming interested*] Is that cotton wool?

OFFICER: [*welcoming the interest, takes the* EXPLORER'*s hand*] Yes certainly! Feel it for yourself — it's specially made for us — that's why it looks different — I'll explain that later. [*A silence whilst the* EXPLORER *takes it all in.*] You are finding it interesting?

EXPLORER: It's a fascinating machine.

OFFICER: When you're interested the heat no longer disturbs you.

EXPLORER: I'm getting used to it.

    [*The* OFFICER *smiles.*]

You were saying the man is strapped in . . .

OFFICER: Yes — as soon as he's strapped in, the bed is set in motion by electric motors — it quivers very minutely from side to side — you must have seen similar instruments in hospitals — it's very precise as the movement corresponds exactly to the harrow which carries out the sentence.

EXPLORER: What exactly is the sentence?

OFFICER: [*amazed*] You didn't know that either! It's disgusting that such an important visitor should not be informed of our methods — I do beg your pardon. You see, the old Commandant always did the explaining, but the new one shirks this duty. However, since I possess the actual drawing made by our former Commandant, I shall be happy to explain the procedure to you.

[*He stops tinkering with the machine, to which he has been making last-minute adjustments from time to time.*]

EXPLORER: The Commandant invented it himself!

OFFICER: [*sharply*] No! The *former* Commandant — not this one — the former Commandant — now dead! [*removes his hat in deference*] Yes, he was a very gifted man — I naturally had a share in it and helped him in the early days with the experiments, but the credit of inventing it belongs entirely to him. [*washes his hands again so as not to soil the drawing*] You've heard of our former Commandant?

EXPLORER: No.

OFFICER: No? Well, it's no exaggeration to say that he created the entire penal settlement — his organization was so perfect that no successor even with a thousand new ideas could change a thing — the new Commandant knows this to be true and has given up trying . . . What a pity you never met the old Commandant — he was a remarkable man . . . ! Our sentence doesn't sound too severe — whatever rule the condemned man breaks is written on his back by the harrow.

EXPLORER: [*referring to the* PRISONER] And his sentence?

OFFICER: "Honour thy superiors!"

[*There is silence.*]

EXPLORER: [*watching the* PRISONER, *who is attempting to understand . . . the* GUARD *is nodding off in the heat*] Does he know his sentence?

OFFICER: [*wishing to continue explanations*] No —

EXPLORER: He doesn't know what's going to happen to him?

OFFICER: No — he'll learn it physically.

[*A silence for the* EXPLORER *to take it in.*]

EXPLORER: But surely he knows he's been *sentenced*?

OFFICER: No, not that either.

EXPLORER: No?

OFFICER: [*anxious to continue*] No!

EXPLORER: Then he didn't know if his defence was effective?

OFFICER: [*turning away in exasperation*] He didn't have a defence.

EXPLORER: But he must have had some chance of defending himself!

OFFICER: [*signals to the* GUARD *to relax — takes the* EXPLORER *by the arm to one side*] You see, I have been appointed judge in the penal settlement despite my youth. [*smiles*] Naturally, as the former Commandant's assistant, I know more about the apparatus than anyone else — my guiding principle is this — Guilt is never to be doubted.
           [*The* EXPLORER *reacts.*]
           I know other courts cannot follow that principle — they have higher courts to scrutinize them who in turn are examined and so on and so forth, but that is not the case here. You'd like me to explain — it's quite simple — the prisoner was assigned on guard duty to the captain — his duty was simply to stand to attention on the stroke of each hour and salute the captain's door — not very exacting, eh? — but very important — he must be alert . . . an enemy could stroll in there — the captain lying asleep! — Last night, as the clock struck two, the captain opened his door and there was his man curled up asleep — so he lashed him across the face with his riding whip, naturally enough. Instead of begging pardon, the prisoner cried: "Throw the whip away or I'll eat you alive" — that's the evidence.

EXPLORER: Did he have a chance to state his version?

OFFICER: [*suppressing his impatience — simply, as to a dolt*] If I had called the man before me for interrogation he would have told lies. If I exposed those lies he would have countered them with another set of lies, and so on and so forth — Everything would become confused, tangled. As it is I've got him and won't let him go. [*smiles*]

EXPLORER: It seems an extraordinary measure to take such

ingenuity and work in devising this machine — just for punishment.

OFFICER: [*smiles*] You must remind yourself that this is a penal settlement and military discipline must be enforced to the last — Is that quite clear? Really, we're wasting time — the execution should commence — [*checks his watch*] — and I've not even finished our guided tour. [*returns to the harrow, puts the* EXPLORER *back in the chair*] As you see, the shape of the harrow corresponds to the human form.

EXPLORER: [*suddenly*] Will the Commandant attend the execution?

OFFICER: Not for certain. [*continuing*] When a man lies down on the bed it begins to vibrate . . .

EXPLORER: [*interrupting*] Doesn't he attend all executions?

OFFICER: [*abruptly*] Much as I dislike to, I must cut all explanations short! Please! Leave it till tomorrow. After the apparatus has been cleaned — its one drawback is that it gets so messy — I'll answer all your questions. Just for now, the essentials . . . The needles are lowered onto his back, barely touching — then the performance begins. As the harrow quivers, its needles pierce the skin of the body, which itself is quivering from the vibration of the bed.

[*The* EXPLORER *shows greater interest.*]

You see, there are two kinds of needle — the long needle does the writing and the short needle sprays a jet of water to wash the blood away and keep the inscription clear. Blood and water are then conducted through this funnel down a waste pipe — into the grave. You can watch the inscription taking place through a glass opening at the top. No trouble was too great for us, you see.

[*By this time the* PRISONER *has dragged the half-asleep* GUARD *over to the machine, where the* PRISONER *has been following the* OFFICER's *movements much as a docile student, but makes no sense of it. The* OFFICER *suddenly turns and sees what is happening, goes to the* GUARD *and kicks him violently up the arse* — *the* GUARD *jerks awake, pulls the* PRISONER *away violently*

          — *the* PRISONER *collapses in a heap, struggling in his chains. The* OFFICER *screams.*]

Get him up! Be careful with him.

          [*He helps the* GUARD *to put the* PRISONER *on his feet.*]

EXPLORER: [*wanting to go*] Thank you . . . Now I know all about it.

OFFICER: [*holding him*] Except for the most important thing — the design. Now, that is regulated according to the inscription — these are the former Commandant's guiding plans. [*takes sheets out of briefcase*] I am afraid they are too precious to let you touch them — I'll hold them up in front of you. [*holds paper in front of the* EXPLORER, *who remains seated*] Read it!

EXPLORER: I don't think I can, it's rather complex.

OFFICER: Yes, it's clear enough.

EXPLORER: It's very ingenious, but I can't make it out.

OFFICER: Yes. [*laughs*] It's not schoolboy calligraphy — it needs to be studied closely, but I'm sure you'd understand it eventually — Of course, the script can't be simple — it's not meant to kill its man immediately — it has six to twelve hours to accomplish that task so there must be lots of flourishes around the actual text — the text itself runs around the body only in a narrow girdle with the rest of the body reserved for embellishments — can you appreciate now the intricate work accomplished by the whole apparatus? — Just watch it.

          [*He goes to the machine and sets it working — it makes the noise of a loud vacuum cleaner and vibrates — one of the sections appears to be making a rasping noise — he shakes his fist at it — he shouts above the noise.*]

Look out — keep to one side! When the needle finishes the first draft of the inscription on his back the body is rolled over, allowing the raw part that has been written on to lie on the cotton wool which absorbs the blood and makes it ready for a deepening of the script — When it rolls over the next time, the teeth at the edge of the harrow tear the cotton wool away from the wounds and so it keeps on writing deeper and deeper for twelve hours. [*stops the machine*] After two hours we take the gag

away as he has no strength left to scream, then he's
given some warm rice pap — as much as his tongue
can lap.

EXPLORER: Can they eat after that?

OFFICER: Not one of them misses the chance! Not in my
experience anyway, and that is pretty extensive.
For the first six hours he only feels pain but retains
appetite — after six hours he loses all desire to eat
— I like to watch this — our man can't swallow his
last mouthful — he only rolls it round and round in
his mouth and then spits it out — I have to duck
then or he'd spit it in my face — and then comes
the moment of enlightenment. [*quiet intensity*] He
begins to understand the inscription — his eyes
tell me first — he radiates — one might even be
tempted to get under the harrow with him — He
deciphers the script with his wounds — you saw
how difficult it was to read with the naked eye, but
our man deciphers it with his wounds, he almost
listens . . . A terribly difficult task, and he needs
six hours to accomplish it — after that the harrow
pierces quite through him, then the soldiers and I
bury him.

[*The* OFFICER *gives a sign to the* GUARD *who tears the*
PRISONER*'s clothes off — he is left in tattered shorts.
The heat seems to hang on everybody like a cloak — the*
PRISONER *is laid on the bed, chains taken off — he's
being strapped on by the* OFFICER *and* GUARD. *All this
is being performed religiously and silently. Suddenly the
wrist-strap breaks.*]

[*mutters*] This is a very complex machine — things
are always breaking here and there — Anyway, this
strap is easily made good — I shall simply use a
chain — it may impair the delicacy of the vibra-
tions, of course — They're so mean at the stores
that if I ask for a new strap they not only take ten
days but ask for the broken one as evidence —
under the former Commandant I had free access to
a grant set aside solely for this purpose — our
present one is always looking for an excuse to
change things — he controls the machine money

personally — How am I supposed to work the machine without a strap? — Nobody bothers about that.

EXPLORER: [*disliking the procedure*] Then the present Commandant is not in sympathy with this procedure?

[*At this moment the* PRISONER *vomits as the* OFFICER *tries to force the gag in his mouth.*]

OFFICER: [*screaming*] It's all the fault of that Commandant — the machine is befouled like a pig-sty.

[*The* GUARD *tries to clean the machine with the* PRISONER'*s shirt.*]

For hours I've told him the prisoner must fast a whole day before execution — But no — the Commandant's lady friends give him chocolate before he's led off — chocolate ... ! Apart from that, who wouldn't be sick chewing a felt gag already slobbered on and gnawed by a hundred dying men? — And yet they won't give me a new one! For three months I've been begging for it! [*takes the* EXPLORER *to one side*] I should like to talk to you in confidence — may I?

EXPLORER: Of course.

OFFICER: This method of execution which you are having the opportunity to admire has at the moment no open supporters in the colony except me — I am its sole advocate trying to uphold the old Commandant's tradition. During his lifetime he had many supporters, but now they skulk out of sight, and now because of the Commandant's new doctrine and the women who whisper to him, is such a piece of work — the work of a lifetime — to fall to disuse ... ? Should we let that happen? Even if one is a stranger here, there is no time to lose — conferences are being held from which I am excluded — an attack of some kind is impending on my function here; you are significant.

EXPLORER: How could I be?

OFFICER: The cowards are using you as a screen — you are a stranger!

EXPLORER: I don't see how ...

OFFICER: [*interrupting*] How different an execution was in the old days ... a whole day before the execution the entire place was packed — we executed outside then — not in a warehouse like criminals! — These few chairs are a miserable reminder to me — they all came to look — the old Commandant appeared with his ladies — fanfare — I, a young cadet then, reported: "Everything in readiness, sir" — the machine glittered — I got spare parts for almost every execution — before hundreds of spectators — all of them standing on tiptoe as far as the eye could see — the condemned man was laid under the harrow by the Commandant himself — and then the execution began! The machine hummed with life — some did not care to watch but listened with closed eyes — they all knew justice was being done — all one heard was the hum and the prisoner's sighs, half muffled by the gag. [*in a moment of sentimental torture*] Aaach! Those long summer afternoons. [*a long silence*] Nowadays the machine can no longer wring a sigh louder than the felt gag can stifle — but in those days the writing needles let drop an acid fluid we're not permitted to use today — Well, then came the sixth hour — the hour of realization — it was impossible to grant the numerous requests to see it close to — the Commandant in his wisdom ordained that the children should have preference — How we absorbed the look of transfiguration on the face of the sufferer — [*gets on his knees*] — the radiance! What times those were, comrade . . .

[*Carried away, the* OFFICER *rests his head against the* EXPLORER. *The* GUARD *has now finished cleaning the machine and is pouring rice into the basin. The* PRISONER *still lies there — he tries to lick up some rice but the* GUARD *withdraws it — it's not his time yet, but puts his dirty hands in and eats some himself.*]

[*pulls himself together*] I'm sorry, I didn't want to upset you — it's impossible to bring those days to life again — don't you see the shame of it?

[*Silence.*]

[*suddenly*] I know what the Commandant is after — he is using you — your verdict against me would increase his power to thwart me. He's calculated it

carefully — he doesn't dare do it himself — no —
he means to use you — an influential foreigner —
this is your second day on the island — you did not
know the old Commandant and his ways — you are
conditioned to European ways of thought and
perhaps you object to capital punishment and
instruments of torture — the public share your
view — the machinery is getting rusty and old —
and perhaps (thinks the Commandant) you disapprove of my methods — and if so, you wouldn't
conceal the fact — Aah! You think, "Why should I
interfere in the customs and peculiarities of a
strange country — this is their way!" But the
Commandant will trick you with sly questions —
an unguarded casual remark will be enough — the
ladies will sit around you and prick up their ears —
you might say in our country a prisoner has a
chance to defend himself — we haven't used
torture since the middle ages, etc. . . . true and
harmless remarks, passing no judgement on my
methods . . . But! I can see our good Commandant
rushing out onto the balcony — his ladies stream-
ing after him — his voice like thunder saying — [*as
if to crowd in square*] "A famous western investigator
studying criminal procedure the world over
condemns our justice as barbaric and inhuman —
this verdict from such a personality makes it
impossible for me to countenance this method any
longer — therefore from this day I ordain . . . etc.
etc. . . " "No!" you may wish to shout out — you
said no such thing — your profound experience
judges my methods to be humane and consonant
with human dignity — too late! You won't even get
onto the balcony — the ladies will hold you back
and close your lips — and I, and the old Commandant, will be done for.

[*Silence.*]

EXPLORER: You overestimate my influence — I'm not an
investigator or even famous — If I gave an opinion
it would be as an individual and therefore be no
more influential than any other ordinary person —
if the Commandant is hostile to your methods then

surely he is strong enough to end your traditions
without help from me . . .

OFFICER: [*shakes his head — low voice*] You don't know the
Commandant — forgive the expression but you
feel like an outsider — yet believe me, your influence cannot be rated too highly! I was delighted
when I heard that you were to attend the execution
without the Commandant — he thought it would
be a blow against me — but I shall turn it to my
advantage . . . You've heard my explanations,
examined the machine and shall watch the execution — any doubt will soon be resolved when you
see it — and now I make this request — Help me
against the Commandant!

EXPLORER: How could I do that? It's impossible — I can
neither help nor hinder you — my influence is
insufficient!

OFFICER: [*becoming frenzied*] Yes you can — you can! I have a
plan — it's bound to succeed — you believe your
influence to be insufficient — I know that it *is* sufficient but even granted that you are right is it not
necessary for the sake of preserving a great tradition to try what may be most difficult? Say nothing
unless you're asked — I don't ask you to lie — by
no means — just be short and formal — such as:
"Yes, I saw the execution — yes, it was explained"
— nothing more — Say you prefer not to discuss
the matter — it would make your blood rise! Of
course, the Commandant will mistake your meaning and put his own interpretation on it . . . That's
the plan — he'll invite you to speak at the
conference tomorrow — this is a public spectacle
that makes me nauseous to take part in — Oh! If for
some mysterious reason you're not invited, you'll
have to ask for an invitation . . . There's no doubt
of your getting it then — you'll even sit in the
Commandant's box with the ladies — various
petty matters will be discussed, mostly harbour
works, nothing but harbour work! So tomorrow
there you are in the Commandant's box — with the
ladies — he keeps looking up to make sure you're
there — then I'll stand up and report that today's

execution has taken place — quite briefly — just a statement — such a statement is not usual, but I'll make it . . . the Commandant thanks me with a smile — and then seizing his opportunity — the opportunity that we have given him — he will say: "I should like to add that this execution was witnessed by a famous foreign investigator who has honoured our colony with his visit — Should we not ask the famous investigator for his verdict on our traditional mode of execution?" Of course, there is loud applause — I clap more loudly than anyone . . . You advance to the front of the box — lay your hands where everyone can see them, or the ladies will squeeze your fingers to distract you — then speak out! (I don't know how I shall endure the tension.) Put no restraint on yourself — publish the truth, loud and clear — lean over the box — shout your convictions — yes indeed, shout! [*waits for reaction from the* EXPLORER] Perhaps that's not in keeping with your character — all right, don't shout — just a few words — whisper even — as long as the officials can hear you — that will be enough — you don't have to mention the lack of funds, the broken strap — the stinking stump of felt! No, I'll take it all on myself — and believe me, if my indictment doesn't drive him out of the assembly hall, it will bring him humbly to his knees — "Yes!" he will cry, "Old Commandant, I humble myself before your memory" . . . This is my plan — you will help me carry it out —

[*The* OFFICER *seizes the* EXPLORER *by his jacket.*]
Of course you will — you must!

[*His shouting has attracted the attention of the* PRISONER *and* GUARD, *who have stopped eating and just stare at him.*]

EXPLORER: [*after a long pause*] No . . . would you like me to explain?

[*The* OFFICER *nods dumbly.*]
I don't approve of your procedure, even before I met you — but I shan't betray what you've told me — I even wondered whether my intervention in this execution would be successful — but I realize

that I must appeal to the Commandant — you've made that fact very clear and since the Commandant is obviously no upholder of this tradition, I imagine my views would be welcome. The very fact that I have been invited to this execution must surely suggest that to you ... I appreciate the sincerity of your convictions, but it can't influence my judgement.

[*The* OFFICER *moves round the machine, numbly checking it. The* EXPLORER *follows him.*]

I shall tell the Commandant what I think — certainly ... but privately, not in public — I am leaving the colony tomorrow, anyway.

OFFICER: [*smiling*] So! You do not find the procedure convincing?

EXPLORER: No — the injustice of the procedure — the inhumanity of the sentence — are undeniable.

OFFICER: You are a stranger here — why should you find it just? If things are different in your country that is a matter of protocol and tradition — but you should not therefore interfere in the methods of a foreign country.

EXPLORER: You expect me to say nothing!

OFFICER: Certainly! You cannot apply your standards to us — nor ours to yours — I will not condemn your country's methods nor interfere — our military and criminal laws are created out of a country's soul and nature: are we not all different? — Each country has a personality almost like a human being — You cannot make me look like you.

EXPLORER: Nor can you make me feel like you.

OFFICER: Of course not!

EXPLORER: But your victim here feels just like all other victims everywhere — they all share the pain.

OFFICER: We are the same — the victim and the oppressor are part of each other — If a country punishes its transgressors it merely smacks its own children who misbehave — It's like a tree — after all — you must hack off rotting or twisting limbs — you do not interfere when you see a gardener do that.

EXPLORER: And if you were a victim you would willingly subject yourself to this?

OFFICER: Yes — even if I were the one healthy limb on a rotting tree. [*long pause*] You're obviously not convinced — Then the time has come . . .

EXPLORER: [*uneasy*] Time for what?

OFFICER: [*excited and brisk; goes to the* PRISONER *and speaks in German*] You're free — yes — you're free.

> [*The* PRISONER'*s face is animated — he cannot believe it — he starts struggling.*]

You'll burst my straps! Lie still — we'll soon loosen them. [*signals the* GUARD *to help*] Draw him out carefully.

> [*They do this — the* PRISONER *is nearly naked. The* OFFICER *goes to the briefcase and takes out the paper with script on it — shows it to the* EXPLORER.]

EXPLORER: I can't — I told you before I can't make out the script.

OFFICER: Take a closer look.

> [*They both stare.*]

No?

EXPLORER: No — not yet.

> [*Trying very hard — the* OFFICER *traces lines on the script with his finger — spells slowly.*]

OFFICER: B . . . E . . . J . . . U . . . S . . . T . . . "Be Just" is what is written there — surely you can read it now.

EXPLORER: [*bends close to the paper*] Maybe . . . I'm prepared to believe you.

OFFICER: Well then . . .

> [*The* OFFICER *puts the paper in the machine — adjusts knobs etc. Seems to be altering the position of the cog wheels. The* GUARD *hands the* PRISONER *his clothes on the end of his bayonet, holding his nose. The* PRISONER *puts his trousers on and washes his shirt in the bucket before putting it on. He and the* GUARD *start giggling at the sight of himself. Happy to find himself of some amusement he turns round — his trousers are split up the back — they both start laughing. The* OFFICER *finishes with the machine — goes to wash his hands — grimaces at the filthy water and wipes his hands on his uniform instead. The* GUARD *and the* PRISONER *suppress laughter. The* OFFICER *surveys the machinery with a smile. He takes the two ladies' handkerchiefs that were tucked in his collar and hands them to the* PRISONER.]

[*to the* PRISONER] Here are your handkerchiefs — a present from the ladies.

[*As the* OFFICER *undresses he handles each garment lovingly — takes a small sword out and breaks it — eventually stands naked — meanwhile, the* GUARD *has snatched the handkerchiefs from the* PRISONER *and they have a friendly wrestle, each trying to possess the handkerchiefs — their attention is now caught by the* OFFICER *as he adjusts the machine to his size and length — a broad grin breaks on the* PRISONER*'s face which remains there. The machine starts vibrating — the* OFFICER *lies on the bed. The* PRISONER, *seeing that the* OFFICER *cannot strap himself in, moves towards the machine. The* GUARD *and the* PRISONER *look at each other, undecided as to who should strap him in. Eventually they both do it. The* PRISONER *jumps round the machine, pointing things out to the* GUARD, *which annoys the* EXPLORER.]

EXPLORER: Go back home.

[*They look uncomprehendingly.*]

Go on — go back home.

[*The* PRISONER, *as if understanding, goes on his knees, appears to be begging to stay — the* EXPLORER *is about to drive him away when the machine starts making a terrible noise — they back away as if it will explode — blood streams down the side of the machine — it is not fulfilling its function.*]

Help me! Turn it off!

[*They all move around the machine, uncertain what to do.*] It's not writing — it's just ripping him! [*finds the switch and turns it off*] Come on — pull him off — take his feet. [*The* OFFICER *is dead — the* EXPLORER *to himself, partly to the* GUARD] He never found his promised redemption — even his apparatus went against him — we must bury him — where's the graveyard?

GUARD: [*speaks for the first time*] You can't bury him there.

EXPLORER: Why not?

GUARD: The priest wouldn't allow the old Commandant to be buried there — so he won't allow the Officer either — they buried the Commandant under a paving stone in the café — "buried like a dog" — he tried several times to dig the old man up at night —

but he was always chased away. The Officer thought he was carrying out a prophecy written on the gravestone.

EXPLORER: What was that?

GUARD: After a number of years the Commandant will rise again and lead his followers into power — have faith and wait.

[*The* EXPLORER *is about to go — turns to the men and distributes a few coins to them and walks off. The* PRISONER *sees his opportunity to snatch back the handkerchiefs — the* GUARD *runs after him. Eventually he takes the handkerchiefs and wears them in the same manner as the* OFFICER. *He puts the* OFFICER'*s hat on and suddenly the* PRISONER *freezes as he sees the shape of his new master.*]

THE END